DOING DIGITAL HISTORY

Manchester University Press

IHR RESEARCH GUIDES

Series editors: Jonathan Blaney, Simon Trafford and Jane Winters
This series is for new researchers in history. By offering a practical introduction to a sub-discipline of history, each book equips its readers to navigate a new field of interest. Every volume provides a survey of the historiography and current research in the subject; describes relevant methodological issues; looks at available primary sources in different media and formats and the problems of their access and interpretation. Each volume includes practical case studies and examples to guide your research, and handy tips on how to avoid some of the pitfalls which may lie in wait for the inexperienced researcher.

The guides are suitable for advanced final-year undergraduates, master's and first-year PhD students, as well as for independent researchers who wish to take their work to a more advanced stage.

Already published
Using film as a source   Sian Barber
History through material culture   Leonie Hannan and Sarah Longair

DOING DIGITAL HISTORY

A BEGINNER'S GUIDE TO WORKING WITH TEXT AS DATA

JONATHAN BLANEY, SARAH MILLIGAN, MARTY STEER AND JANE WINTERS

Manchester University Press

Copyright © Jonathan Blaney, Sarah Milligan, Marty Steer and Jane Winters 2021

The right of Jonathan Blaney, Sarah Milligan, Marty Steer and Jane Winters to be identified as the authors of this work has been asserted by them in accordance with the Copyright, Designs and Patents Act 1988.

Published by Manchester University Press
Altrincham Street, Manchester M1 7JA

www.manchesteruniversitypress.co.uk

British Library Cataloguing-in-Publication Data
A catalogue record for this book is available from the British Library

ISBN   978 1 5261 3268 0   paperback

First published 2021

The publisher has no responsibility for the persistence or accuracy of URLs for any external or third-party internet websites referred to in this book, and does not guarantee that any content on such websites is, or will remain, accurate or appropriate.

Typeset by
Servis Filmsetting Ltd, Stockport, Cheshire

CONTENTS

List of figures	*page* vii
List of tables	ix
Acknowledgements	xi
Glossary	xiii
Introduction	1
1 The context of digital history	5
2 Formulating your research questions	26
3 How a digital project begins	48
4 Working with text 1: unstructured text	58
5 Working with text 2: structured text	90
6 Caring for your digital history project	106
7 Visualising your data	123
8 What next for digital history?	149
Test yourself answers	157
Appendix 1: Getting the data	159
Appendix 2: Some command line recipes	161
Appendix 3: Regular expressions	165
References	166
Index	172

FIGURES

3.1	Blenheim Road in *The Post Office London Directory for 1879*	*page* 49
4.1	Sublime Text	64
4.2	The Ball's Pond Road `.txt` file in Sublime Text with all numbers highlighted by regex search for `[0-9]`	66
4.3	Addition of 'House number' in Sublime Text using regex find (`^[0-9]+`) replace `House number $1`	69
4.4	The command line	70
4.5	The default Mac Terminal	72
4.6	Git Bash	72
4.7	Folder contents shown by `ls`	74
4.8a-b	The results of `grep "1" Balls-Pond-road.txt`	76
4.9	The results of `grep -Eo "^[13579]+" Balls-Pond-road.txt`	79
4.10a-b	The results of `grep -Eo "^[0-9]*[13579] " Balls-Pond-road.txt`	80
4.11	The results of `grep -Eo "^[0-9]*[13579] " Balls-Pond-road.txt	less`	83
4.12	The results of `grep -Ev "^[0-9]+" Balls-Pond-road.txt`	86
4.13	The results of `grep -E "^[0-9]" *.txt	grep -v ","	less`	87
5.1	The results of `grep "Mr" *.xml	grep -v "Mrs"`	93
5.2	The results of `grep -E "\bMiss\b" all-b-streets.xml	grep -E "\bMrs\b"`	96
5.3	The results of `grep "<addr>" all-b-streets.xml	grep -E "\bMrs\b|\bMiss\b"	grep -Eo ",[^,]+</addr>"`	98

7.1	Top ten female professions	135
7.2	Top female married and unmarried professions	136
7.3	First attempt to understand the visualisation task	143
7.4	Placing indicative buildings onto the map	144
7.5	The finished visualisation in greyscale	146

TABLES

4.1	Common file formats	*page* 61
4.2	Quantifiers in regular expressions	66
4.3	The most useful `grep` flags	81
4.4	`Grep` results for commercial and residential properties	85
6.1	Creative Commons licence types	121
A2.1	Some command line recipes	161
A3.1	Summary of regular expression characters	165

ACKNOWLEDGEMENTS

For their expertise and patience, we would like to thank our colleagues in the Institute of Historical Research's Wohl Library: Mette Lund, Ceri Thompson, Michael Townsend and Kate Wilcox; and Clare George and Jordan Landes from Senate House Library. Gabriel Bodard, Philip Carter, Kunika Kono and Nicky Old gave us help and advice at various stages of writing.

Adam Chapman, Jessica Davies-Porter, Hannah Elias, Danny Millum, Olwen Myhill and Julie Spraggon read and commented on draft chapters; they corrected errors, pointed out inconsistencies and cut some questionable jokes. Naturally all that remain are our own.

We would like to thank the anonymous reader of the manuscript, whose thorough and thoughtful comments led us to think again about almost all of the text.

Emma Brennan, our editor at MUP, was encouraging and patient while the book was being written. At a crucial stage we benefited greatly from her editorial skill and insight as she helped us to reshape the structure we had started out with so that it actually worked. Joe Haining copy-edited the manuscript with both sympathy and rigour, making the book more consistent, more readable and helped us to make some complex ideas easier to follow.

Special thanks are due to Andrew Frow, who generously supplied us with the digital map on which our Beaufort Street visualisation is based, from his own collection. Most of all, we are grateful to our colleague Simon Baker of the Bibliography of British and Irish History, who over many years has kept us supplied with more just-published digital history references than we knew what to do with.

GLOSSARY

| | see **pipe**
add in **Git** | to mark files to be included in the next **commit**
anchor | one of two **regular expression** characters meaning either the beginning or end of a line
API (application programming interface) | a facility offered by a web resource which allows complex querying and download of search results; API queries can sometimes be done by manipulating the URL but are usually carried out by scripts written in any programming languages allowed by the API
attribute | part of an XML **element** which, paired with a **value**, extends the encoding; for example, in <person married="yes"> the attribute is married and its value is yes
bash | the program run by default in the **command line**, and so often a synonym for command line
big data | lots of data, usually updated in real time in a constant stream, sufficiently large to be beyond the analytical capacity of standard software
bitonal | a scanning format using only black and white, meaning that gradations and detail are lost but the file is smaller than with **greyscale**
born digital | data which was created in digital format
branch in **Git** | create a separate copy of the files in a **repository** to do work away from the principal work, for example by experimenting
cat (concatenate) | a command line instruction to list the contents of a file or files
cd (change directory) | a command line instruction to move to a specified folder

character class	a set of characters in a **regular expression**, any one of which may match
check out	change a file in a **Git repository** to a different, usually earlier, version
CLI (command line interface)	see **command line**
clone	take a complete copy of a **Git repository** using the command Git clone
command line	a text interface for interacting with a computer, see also **bash**, **CLI**, **terminal**
commit	create a snapshot of files in a **Git repository**, so that they can be reverted to that version
crowdsourcing	an open invitation to the public to enrich a resource, for example by providing or correcting transcriptions from images
CSV (comma-separated values)	a structured text format in which commas designate columns
distant reading	a computational approach to collections of texts which aims to identify aggregate patterns
DTD (document type definition)	a rules file for **XML** that is less powerful than a **schema** but simpler to write
element	a complete piece of **XML markup**, usually consisting of two **tags**
flag	a modification to the default command line instruction, normally preceded by a hyphen; for example, `grep -i` makes grep case insensitive
geocoding	the process of associating an object with a map location
georectification	the process of altering a historic map so that it aligns with a modern map of the same part of the earth's surface
GIS (Geographic Information System)	a system for interfacing geographical data with a map display
Git (see also **version control**)	a program which keeps track of changes in files and can revert them to an earlier state; the files are usually kept on a personal computer and in a cloud **repository** and synched between the two
grep (global regular expression print)	a **command line** program for searching **plain text** files

greyscale	a scan which preserves the gradations of the original but in monochrome, leading to higher quality and higher file sizes than the **bitonal** format
hash (for **hash value**)	a representation of a file as a fixed number of digits, used in **version control** and in ensuring files have not been tampered with; the algorithms which produce hashes ensure that the smallest changes to a file change the hash completely
HTML (Hypertext Markup Language)	a structured text format for presenting documents in a web browser
JSON (JavaScript Object Notation)	a structured text format
Linux	a free operating system based on the earlier Unix operating system
machine-readable	text capable of being understood by a program as text, as opposed to a photograph of some text, which is understood as a sequence of pixels
markup	instructions for how the content of a file should be processed or understood; the commonest markup languages are **HTML**, which gives instructions for how a file should be displayed in a web browser, and **XML**, which describes how the contents of a file are structured and what that structure means
merge	in **Git**, unify multiple **branches** and, where there are conflicts, make decisions about which part of which file to prefer
neural network	a computerised attempt to mimic the way the human brain is structured and learns
OCR (optical character recognition)	a programmatic transcription of an image of text (cf. **rekeying**)
pipe	the command line syntax |, pronounced pipe, which sends the output of the command before the pipe to the command after the pipe
plain text	text in a format where presentational information, if it exists, does not change the appearance of the text on screen, for example bold text is not shown as bold but with an instruction to make it bold; plain text files often have the extension .txt (cf. **WYSIWYG**)

GLOSSARY

precision — in search results, the percentage of results which are correct (cf. **recall**)

pwd (print working directory) — a command line instruction to give the current location

quantifier — a **regular expression** character which stipulates how many times the preceding character must be found in order to match

RDF (resource description framework) — a model for structuring information in sets of triples, taking the form *subject, object, predicate*

recall — in search results, the percentage of correct search results from the total correct results in the collection searched (cf. **precision**)

regex — see **regular expression**

regular expression — a syntax for searching (and optionally replacing) text based on patterns of characters; see Appendix 3 for a summary of the syntax

rekeying — a human transcription of an image of text (cf. **OCR**)

repository — a collection of files under **version control** using **Git**

schema — a rules file for XML written in XML, more powerful than a **DTD** but more complex to write

shapefile — a format for describing an area or natural feature so that it can be used in digital mapping

string — a sequence of characters: *how are you?* including the punctuation and spaces, is a string

tag — part of an **XML element**, usually in opening and closing pairs, but sometimes standing alone

TEI (Text Encoding Initiative) — a set of guidelines for encoding texts in **XML**

terminal — a synonym for **command line**

text editor — a program which displays files in plain text format, as opposed to an editor like Microsoft Word, which shows only the effect (**WYSIWYG**)

TSV (tab-separated values) — a structured text format in which tabs designate columns

GLOSSARY xvii

Unix an operating system developed by Bell Labs which is in large part the basis of the Mac and Linux operating systems; the Windows operating system has a different basis

value part of an XML **element** which, paired with a **attribute**, extends the encoding; for example in `<person married="yes">`, the value of the attribute `married` is `yes`

version control a system for tracking the state of a set of files over time and reverting to different states if required. The commonest system in use is **Git**

Web 2.0 the form of the web which allows users to add their own content to a website, for example in blog comments and social media posts

WYSIWYG (What You See is What You Get) an editor which shows a document in a presentational format, for example bold text appears bold on screen; Microsoft Word is the most commonly used WYSIWYG editor (cf. **plain text**)

XML (Extensible Markup Language) a flexible language for marking up text according to the choice of the user

XML editor an editor capable of understanding XML syntax, comparing it to the rules given in an associated **DTD** or **schema**, and reporting errors

INTRODUCTION

This book is a practical guide for using digital tools and techniques for historical research, but it should be useful for anyone from across the humanities who is interested in working with collections of texts at scale. We do focus on text and so, although our examples will be historical, their applicability to the study of literature, for example, should be evident.

This book is aimed at non-programmers and it does not teach or require the use of any programming language. The practical examples we work through substantiate our belief that you can do a great deal without programming, by leveraging the work of others. Learning to program is interesting and useful but it is not essential to doing digital history and many digital historians choose not to. There are certainly things that can only be done with coding but we have purposely omitted all such things. We hope you will be surprised by the power and flexibility of the approaches we show you.

We have deliberately chosen to focus almost entirely on tools which have been used for decades and which we expect to continue to be used for many more years. They are mature and there is an abundance of advice available online to supplement what we show in the book.

We do insist that much of the work in digital history projects is likely to consist in preparing the data for the interesting part of the project: the part that produces interesting results (whether that be an idea, a graph, a map or a website). This is often known as 'data cleaning'. Actually, that term is slightly misleading because it implies that the problems with the underlying data are always errors of some kind. Sometimes the data needed for a project arrives in a clean and well-organised condition, but simply happens to be in the wrong format for its new use and so requires preparatory work. Data preparation is not much discussed when digital projects are written up, but this book is a practical guide and so we have tried to give it due prominence.

Our book follows the general structure of other volumes in the IHR Research Guides series. Chapter 1, 'The context of digital history', describes the history of our subject and some of its milestones. What is available as a digital source, and how, is a product of the history of the subject and, more importantly, early drivers of digitisation, such as the commercial value of genealogical sources. In writing this chapter we found it hard to disentangle digital history from the digital humanities more broadly considered and we suggest that trying to impose a clear demarcation is unhelpful.

Chapter 2, 'Formulating your research questions', will help you to think through your research ideas in the context of digital history. What techniques will you need? What is already available in terms of data and tools? A critical and judicious approach to early decisions here (both in terms of the research project you pursue and any resources you employ) can save you valuable time and energy and we give lots of advice on how to make those decisions. The last section may seem to skip ahead to some thoughts on where and how you might publish your research. We think that it is best to have a rough idea of this from the very beginning and we also suggest that you should not think of publishing solely in terms of final outputs.

Chapter 3, 'How a digital project begins', is a nuts-and-bolts discussion of how a research project might go from books on a shelf to digital output. In our experience not many people are confident with the process of digitising material because they have no experience of doing so. This chapter describes that process. We digitised part of a book specifically for *Doing digital history* and have made our files freely available online (see Appendix 1). The book is *The Post Office London Directory for 1879*, and we have tried to use it for our historical questions and for our practical examples wherever we could throughout the book.

Chapters 4 and 5 go into detail on how to work with digitised text automatically and at scale. We show how you can use the *command line*, which gives you access to hundreds of small programs written by other people, and with which you can accomplish an enormous amount without writing a line of code. We make no apology for talking at length about the command line: it is the Swiss army knife of computing, beloved of most programmers. Learning even a little bit about how to use the command line can transform the way you work. Plain text is covered in Chapter 4 and structured text in Chapter 5. We will show that plain text is harder to deal with, although perhaps easier to get hold of, and that structured text is preferable when available, even if at first glance its appearance may be more forbidding. For structured text we concentrate on XML

(Extensible Markup Language), but the approaches we take should transfer reasonably easily to other formats.

Chapter 6, 'Caring for your digital history project', covers the practicalities of managing your data and sharing it effectively. Our section on research data management spends a fair amount of time on using the Git tool to manage your data, because we think this is simply the best option available. Further, a great deal of reusable data can now be found in the form of a Git repository, so a basic understanding of what that means and how it works is becoming essential. We also look at documentation and metadata.

Chapter 7, 'Visualising your data', gives an overview of visualising historical data with some advice on practical aspects, such as the use of colour. Here we use the Post Office data to create some visualisations of our own, in the form of charts and a map, with detailed information on how we went from dataset to visualisation and why we made the choices that we did.

Chapter 8, 'What next for digital history?', is our attempt to predict what new technologies are around the corner for historians and how they might affect your work. This chapter ignores George Eliot's advice, in *Middlemarch*, that 'of all forms of mistake, prophecy is the most gratuitous'. We hope that, even if this chapter eventually proves to be laughably wrong in some of the details, the generalities will affect historical practice one way or another. We put the finishing touches to this book while much of the world was in lockdown because of the COVID-19 pandemic. We have not revised our predictions, even though our expectation of 'gradual evolution and embedding rather than of revolution and disruption' already looks dated. We think it is too early to say what long-term changes the pandemic will bring to the practice of history.

We have also included three appendices: Appendix 1 describes the data repository we have created for this book – what is in it, how to get a copy of it and how you might want to use it to practise your skills. Appendix 2 is a table of command line tools and how to use them. We give a human-language description of what each command does and some more extended examples of how you can use them for common tasks. We hope this will be a useful ready reference for day-to-day command line work. Appendix 3 is a summary of the syntax of regular expressions. We think getting to grips with regular expressions, or regex, is essential for working digitally with text. We introduce regular expressions bit by bit in Chapter 4, but Appendix 3 provides a convenient summary in one place. Regular expressions are not easy to learn but we encourage you to keep practising and referring back to this appendix any time you need to.

There are many things we have not included in this book. Equally, our readers do not need to master everything we do cover. Digital history has many facets, some more appropriate to a particular field or congenial to a particular researcher than others. If this book encourages some historians to try something new or go further with a digital approach than they had previously then it will have been worth writing.

1

THE CONTEXT OF DIGITAL HISTORY

INTRODUCTION

It is a difficult task, doomed in advance, to say in a few words what has really changed in our area of study, and especially how and why that change took place.[1]

There are a number of strands we have to try to weave together in describing the context and development of digital history. We will start by discussing the place of digital history within the broader context of digital humanities, and then within the context of the development of technology in the post-war period. We will move on to discussing the effect of the digital on three areas of the historian's craft: finding, writing and citing.

A sceptical view of the impact of digital history might suggest that it only really involves traditional historical methods speeded up. It would be possible, for example, for a team of researchers over many years to read the whole of Hansard and create an index of the appearance of a particular term or set of terms; now one researcher can do the same thing in a leisurely morning's work. But, as we will see in Chapter 2, the digitisation of Hansard has led to much deeper change in historical work. Speed, moreover, changes things by itself. The digital has changed life fundamentally for historians and, as there are trade-offs with all change, these changes are not uniformly positive. We will look at the effects of technological developments, but this will not be simply a celebration of digital approaches. Digital offers extra tools for the historian's toolbox, not replacements for the old ones.

A broader point, which we will touch on only here, is that the fundamental changes engendered by the digital have not just affected historians but indeed all of us. It has changed how plumbers, surgeons, schoolchildren, till operators and parents carry out their tasks and so has changed them as people.[2] Historians, then, are just one more group carried along by changes in society. Some commentators, like Nicholas Carr and Matthew Crawford, are concerned that the effect on society is overall a negative one, particularly in terms of the skills such as reading and reasoning which are central to historical research.[3]

Just as the analogue world has not gone away, and smartphones can be switched off when walking in the countryside, so the working world of the historian is not wholly digital and we hope and expect that it never will be. The catalogue terminal still very frequently leads us to books and to manuscripts; the web leads to new opportunities to meet other historians, to visit archives, libraries and museums. At its best, the digital world can be a finding aid to what we really value.

DIGITAL HUMANITIES AND DIGITAL HISTORY

Much has been written and debated around the definition of digital humanities.[4] This book is a practical guide to doing digital history and so not the place to revisit those debates. But we do want to insist on one thing: doing digital humanities need not involve writing programs (also known as coding).[5] We would be committed to this proposition even if this book, which contains no coding, was not an attempt to instantiate it. Digital humanities, in our view, is a question of approach: if you are actively and critically using digital tools to aid your work in researching, teaching or learning, you are probably doing digital humanities. We would encourage anyone to learn to program if they are interested in doing so, but we do not see it as a defining characteristic of work in digital humanities.[6]

The overlap between digital humanities and digital history is large. Many techniques are common to both and few historical resources are unexploited by researchers from other disciplines. For example, Early English Books Online (EEBO) is a commercial project which provides page scans of books published in England or English between 1472 and 1700.[7] The books digitised by EEBO are of great interest to historians, but also to scholars of literature, theology, art history, linguistics, law and many other subjects.[8] With twenty-five thousand transcriptions now available from the academic consortium EEBO-TCP, many researchers from different disciplines are able to use this corpus to do the aggregate work which is one feature of digital humanities. Digital resources many times smaller than EEBO are also of use to researchers across the humanities, and any bright line between digital history and digital humanities is of questionable value.

The Spanish historian Anaclet Pons divides the history of what we now call digital humanities into three eras:

1. The 'heroic' era of work by pioneers
2. Pre-web work when computers were becoming widespread and the field was known as 'humanities computing'
3. The web-enabled digital humanities era, characterised by abundance[9]

Before we even get to the pioneers of the computing age, a literary example of work that would now be done by computing is T. C. Mendenhall's 'The characteristic curves of composition' (1887). As described by Geoffrey Rockwell and Stéphan Sinclair, Mendenhall produced graphs of word length frequencies for authors in an attempt to prove that Francis Bacon wrote the works of Shakespeare.[10] This was not the first visualisation by any means – William Playfair, working in the eighteenth century, is credited by the *Oxford Dictionary of National Biography* as the inventor of 'three fundamental forms of statistical graph – the time-series line graph, the bar chart, and the pie chart'[11] – but it is a striking echo of work done today. To prove the point, Rockwell and Sinclair have recreated Mendenhall's work in a downloadable Jupyter notebook.[12]

However, the first of the early digital humanists proper was probably Josephine Miles. A scholar of English poetry, particularly of the seventeenth century, Miles pioneered computational approaches to literature. Most notably, she worked on a concordance (an alphabetical index to all the words used in a work, used as a finding aid) to the poetry of John Dryden using punched cards and early computers.[13] Miles commented pithily on this process and its advantages:

> Three problems were primary: the bulk of the work, the cost of publication, the difficulty of accurate checking by assistants unfamiliar with the material. The decision to use IBM machines as an aid in checking helped solve the other problems in turn.[14]

Better known, but slightly later, is the work of Roberto Busa. He used an IBM computer to make possible the indexing of the voluminous works of Thomas Aquinas. Appropriately, the output of this project, the *Index Thomisticus*, followed a sequence found with many long-lived digital humanities projects: it was published first as a multi-volume print edition, then as a CD-ROM, followed ultimately by a web version.[15]

The beginnings of digital history itself are strongly associated with two historical movements: the quantitatively focused and largely American *cliometrics* movement and the French *Annales* school. Cliometrics lends itself particularly to questions of economic history and population history, placing great value on statistical methods and approaches. The article 'The economics of slavery in the antebellum South' by Alfred Conrad and John Meyer, published in 1958, is a foundational document for cliometrics' mathematical approach to historical questions. Here Conrad and Meyer argue that, absent the US Civil War, slavery would have continued in the South, because it was profitable. The novelty of the paper, however, lay in their methodology rather than their conclusion. The authors tested their 'hypothesis' by examining data including prices for slaves and cotton, output per slave, life expectancy and reproduction rates among slaves (the language of the article is studiedly neutral on the horrors that lay behind the figures). Interestingly, given that a theme of our chapter is the way that wider technological change influenced historical practice, a criticism Conrad and Meyer make of previous approaches to this question is that:

> the debate over the value of the different constituent pieces of information reconstructs in embryo much of the historical development of American accounting practices.[16]

Annales historians, although they differ somewhat in approach and interests, have focused on the *longue durée* of economic and social history and so, as with advocates of cliometrics, naturally took an early interest in how computing could make this work less labour intensive. Perhaps the most enthusiastic of the group was Emmanuel Le Roy Ladurie, who was clear that computers are not simply labour-saving devices, but that they altered the direction of historical study: where previously 'the massive extent of the documents seems to have paralysed researchers', now (he was writing in 1970), 'modern techniques ... permit a genuine historiographical revolution'.[17]

An early example of the use of computing in British historical research was the work of Roderick Floud. While doing doctoral research in 1965, Floud obtained extensive historical records from an engineering firm and used a computer to analyse the vast quantity of material he had acquired. It is probably relevant that, as well as being an economic historian, Floud was a proponent of quantitative and econometric history: early historical work using computers often had to focus tightly on number crunching because computers were primarily designed for this function at that time. Floud recalls that, while there was hostility to cliometrics itself among some historians, this did not extend to the use of computers: 'computing ... was really seen as being a natural extension of other forms of historical scholarship'.[18]

This distinction of Floud's makes it difficult to disentangle much of the criticism of computational approaches to history which was published in the next couple of decades. The actual target seems often to be the use of statistics as methodologically central, rather than the use of computers as a tool to handle the volume of statistics being studied.[19] But, without wishing to labour the point, it is the tool which allows the work, and in this area of historical research we should not neglect the influence of everyday tools such as the desktop calculator.[20]

The Association for History and Computing was founded in the United Kingdom in 1987 and its journal, *History and Computing*, styling itself a magazine, was published from 1989. The first number was divided into 'Feature articles', 'Education', 'Hardware, software and courseware' and 'Book reviews'. Feature articles included a description of the use of a database to analyse the social basis of a progressive movement in nineteenth-century Portugal and a statistical analysis of English parliamentary elections using Hertford poll books, using a spreadsheet program.[21] The two sections on education and tools are illustrative of how new the approach was to many historians, and also of a commendably welcoming approach to interested newcomers. This environment, offering a generous welcome to all, with no assumption of prior knowledge, has been continued by some digital history publications, such as the tutorial website *The Programming Historian*.[22]

TECHNOLOGICAL CHANGE

Historians are also shaped by their desktop tools and applications, and here they also largely use tools that were not designed for historians but for quite other uses. Microsoft Office, as its name implies, tries to replace elements of the traditional office with software: Word and Outlook instead of a typing pool; Excel instead of account clerks; PowerPoint instead of a reprographics specialist. But as these jobs have been lost, the skills of those who did them have been inadequately replaced.[23] Word invites us all to become typesetters, and a glance at almost any Word document reveals that we actually need to be trained to do that. Indeed, the very paper that we use for printing documents, A4, is a poor choice, because it was intended for handwriting at much larger letter size. Compare an academic book with a standard A4 Word document and you will find the former is much easier to read and digest. A4 paper is the right size for handwriting, and for that reason the wrong size for single-column print.[24] Habit, and some degree of technological lock-in, subtly shape historians' work in ways which are rarely questioned or evaluated.[25] Anaclet Pons rightly warns us that we should not lose sight of the profound effect these tools have in fact had:

> We have internalised them as everyday resources, as if we had always enjoyed them, as if they were quite natural and had not completely changed our profession's way of working.[26]

We can look to the availability of tools on desktop computers to help explain the rise of certain techniques in digital history. To take two examples from data visualisation, which we shall discuss in Chapter 7, Excel comes equipped with a number of default charting tools, where data can be visualised at the click of a button and rendered differently at the click of another. Many articles that contain graphs and charts are, quite reasonably, generated in just this way. A further steer towards using Excel's native visualisation tools is that many humanities journals require submission in a format similar to or solely in Word. The interoperability between the two programs means that it is easier to work with visualisations in Word that come from Excel than from elsewhere. We say this not to condemn users of Microsoft Office but simply to note the constraints that tools bring with them: Excel offers only a limited type and style of data visualisation. Thus, the tool inevitably shapes what historians are producing.

Excel may also be linked to the rise in interest among historians of network diagrams and the techniques of social network analysis pioneered by social scientists. The network software Gephi, which first appeared in 2008, is often considered by humanities researchers to be more user-friendly than the alternatives which were available before then.[27] Gephi's ability to import data directly from Excel means that those researchers can prepare their data in a form they are already quite familiar with rather than having to learn another format. Had Gephi, or something similar, not appeared as free and accessible piece of software, then might we have seen fewer articles published about historical networks?

This is just one of many possible examples of the way that technological change can affect historical practice. Software is preferred if it allows historians with limited time for training to begin to use it and see some results fairly quickly, and thus assess if further time investment is worthwhile. This may seem common sense but it does shape historical practice, especially through the quotidian tools which are most likely to be taken for granted.

Improvements in hardware, such as the standard desktop computer, can make techniques such as video editing or 3D work much more widely available than previously, because the processing power or graphics capabilities required were not available on office equipment. Any move from specialist hardware to general equipment will make casual experimentation more likely. For example, some digital humanities centres or 'labs' are now able to buy 3D printers for exploratory work rather than with specific project funding.[28]

In terms of the availability of information, we begin to see the emergence of a qualitative difference between digital history approaches to different historical periods. In medieval history there is a relatively small amount of data, much of which is textual. Although far too much for any individual to assimilate, it does mean that the corpus, while large, is approachable with digital tools. By contrast, a twentieth-century historian faces a relative abundance of data, in many media, including audio and video. As well as posing problems of just how such a mass can be sifted, a topic we return to in Chapter 2, a great deal of material is still in copyright and may not only be difficult to access but also to analyse and reproduce. Historians of the twenty-first century will, given the exponential increase in digital data, find these difficulties much exacerbated.[29]

As we have seen, there is a pattern of digital history gradually expanding into areas that were previously prohibitive in terms of equipment. We will give one further example: *big data*. Big data has a number of definitions but here we can think of it as data that is derived from a large stream of real-world information that is continually updated. Meteorologists are intensive users of big data, using enormous amounts of computing power to process it and produce, among other things, the five-day weather forecast. There is a cachet, or a swagger, about big data, making it a useful term to drop into the inflated vocabulary of funding applications, and which has led D'Ignazio and Klein, in *Data Feminism*, to call it 'Big Dick Data'.[30]

A humanities example of big data would be the archiving and analysis of Twitter data around a specific event, such as the UK's 2016 referendum on membership of the European Union. Such an archive would be a valuable primary source for historians but it is a difficult dataset to deal with at scale, as the travails of the Library of Congress's ambitious plan to archive all of Twitter have shown.[31] There are costs not only in processing the information but in acquiring it from Twitter in the first place (access to large amounts of Twitter data is not free). But the benefits of such a rich primary source are obvious: a large, admittedly self-selecting, group of individuals (or possibly the automated accounts known as bots) commenting on a historical event in real time. For example, after the terrorist attacks in Paris in 2015, a team of French scholars tried to archive reactions to the events, not just on Twitter but on the web in general.[32] This was extremely useful work, but it required a team of researchers already equipped, skilled and able to react immediately.

Twitter is just one part of the web. What about the rest of it? You may be aware of the valiant attempt to archive the public web, by the Internet Archive, which began archiving snapshots of websites, along with much else, in 1996. The Internet Archive is a charity and not directly affiliated with any government archives or libraries. Over time it increased the scale of its collection and the frequency of its snapshots of individual sites which are now accessible through the Wayback Machine.[33]

This is, or was, a strange state of affairs: that only a sole organisation, a charity, would be archiving the most important publication medium of our time. However, at least in some prosperous countries the national 'domain' (a country's part of the web) is now being archived by a national web archive. In the UK this is done by the British Library, on behalf of the six UK copyright libraries.[34] The UK web domain, which in itself is not an easy to thing to determine, is periodically *crawled* (systematically searched and indexed) and archived. Only the public web, by which we mean sites not behind a paywall or access controls such as an intranet, is captured. Additionally, there are thematic, curated collections around key events.[35]

What are the implications of this huge UK dataset for historians? It is early days, but some exploratory work has been done.[36] There are varying degrees of access to different web archives: some might be usable directly from a browser anywhere in the world; some may be accessible only within an archive; others may be effectively closed to researchers. Each web archive has the responsibility to build tools, so varying resources and priorities may mean that features available to users, like what kinds of search fields are available, will vary greatly.

A key finding from early work on the UK Web Archive by historians and other humanities researchers illustrates the difficulties in working through the sheer quantity of data available. The text search interface to the archive will find many thousands of results for all but the most obscure keyword search; users should not and cannot expect results ordered by 'relevance', in the familiar way that Google tailors its search results for each individual user. New strategies are clearly required and it is early days for researchers in adapting their approach.[37]

There is no sign that this trend towards increasing abundance is slowing. Historians, whatever their period or subject, will have to adapt their approaches and skills to compensate.

FINDING

Whether in areas of abundance or scarcity, the most dramatic effect of the digital on the historian is the ease of finding. Reading and writing may be enabled (or hindered) by being in digital form but they are not many orders of magnitude faster in the way that search allows initial discovery to be.

A prophetic text in the history of technology is the engineer Vannevar Bush's 'As we may think'. In the 1930s, Bush saw that computers could be much more than a machine for processing numbers – they could bring together multiple information sources through a kind of hyperlink. Bush named the environment he imagined as a 'memex', and he saw it as being as useful to the historian as to the scientist:

> The historian, with a vast chronological account of a people, parallels it with a skip trail which stops only on the salient items, and can follow at any time contemporary trails which lead him all over civilization at a particular epoch. There is a new profession of trail blazers, those who find delight in the task of establishing useful trails through the enormous mass of the common record.[38]

Textual resources, such as digital libraries, which seem inevitable to us today, were foreseen by the American scientist J. C. R. Licklider in his 1965 book *Libraries of the Future*. He argued that libraries would become 'precognitive' network computers. These ideas derived from the principles of cybernetics (information storage, retrieval, human organisation and control systems), which is turn is based on mathematical models of communication and network theories.[39]

In contrast to the scholarly, or even otherworldly, projects of indexing Dryden or Aquinas, for-profit digitisation with full-text search began in earnest in the 1970s as companies, such as LexisNexis, responded to the needs of legal research. As Tim Hitchcock, who researches crime and punishment, explains, the legal system in the West is 'synonymous with the use of digital search tools'.[40] He goes on to explore the consequences of the digitisation of legal texts being carried out primarily for law firms, secondarily for family historians and scarcely at all for academic historians. Here Hitchcock identifies an important feature of digital history: commercial preferences have largely determined what has been digitised and, almost as importantly, how it has been digitised.

The publishing trajectory of *Index Thomisticus*, described above, was followed by some major resources of use to historians. Before internet access was widespread, print works such as *The Bibliography of British and Irish History* (then known as the *Royal Historical Society Bibliography*) and the *Oxford English Dictionary* (*OED*) appeared first on CD-ROM, and were only later transformed into web resources. In the case of *The Bibliography of British and Irish History*, listings were first published from 1909 in book form, with thematic volumes supplemented by annual updates across all material within the bibliography's scope. Although immensely valuable as a tool, the book form was slow to update and inevitably scattered relevant references (for example, the works of the same author) across numerous books. Search was limited to the organisation of the individual volume, which necessarily varied from one to the next, and the index (long-run print projects are characterised almost inevitably by inconsistency). *The Royal Historical Society Bibliography on CD-ROM*, published in 1995, ameliorated only the search problems; updates naturally remained difficult. The perceived uneasiness of historians with non-print materials is evident in the printed booklet included in the case, which contains descriptions of the taxonomy and a history of the project. This supporting material might easily have gone on the CD-ROM itself.[41]

Genealogical resources, much more commercially successful instruments than these scholarly tools, were also published on disc in the pre-internet period: Ancestry, a huge online subscription corpus, had its digital antecedents in distributed floppy discs and CD-ROMs. Although the audience for these resources is different, the shaping effect of the popularity of family history research on digital history is clear. Independent family historians often develop impressive research skills, but their needs and interests are distinct from those of academic historians. For now, the point to note is that what has been digitised gains disproportionately more attention than what has not.

Most influential of all the commercial services, Google Books began digitising in 2004, working in partnership with university libraries to digitise their printed collections and make them freely available online. Although the project was not novel (the Gutenberg Project began in 1971; the Internet Archive in 1996), the scale and name recognition of Google Books is unrivalled. Google's aim with the project was fast, large-scale digitisation, and it has succeeded in making millions of books available in different forms, broadly according to their copyright status. Google's purpose was not to meet the needs of scholars but, we can reasonably assume, to maintain or extend its dominance of web search. Given this, it might seem a category error by scholars to complain that Google Books does not meet their needs: it is not designed to meet their needs. But in the real world, historians use Google Books and Google Books does have important limitations and drawbacks: its metadata is often inadequate for serious research; the variability of access (some books are wholly available, some in snippets, and some not at all) biases what gets read and what does not. Most fundamentally, Google is a commercial operation which can, and does, change anything about its products without asking the permission of academics. Regardless, Google Books is now part of the ecology of historical research and, like a vigorous invasive species, its presence has effects on the whole ecosystem.

Keyword searching of thousands or millions of books or newspapers allows a well-constructed search to turn up textual evidence that simply would not have been found by historians reading through print or microfilmed text. One effect of this, as practised by historian Dan Cohen, is that this is a democratising process: close reading privileges a small canon of works, but *distant reading*, as this aggregate process is known, is far broader and can take in, say, nineteenth-century texts of all kinds.[42]

Many historians have raised questions about the effect that reading via keyword search has on the contextual knowledge of historians. We can vividly imagine reading a nineteenth-century newspaper as its original readers would have and can see that jumping via search to an item and reading it in isolation robs us of much contextual knowledge. Where was the item on the page? What other articles or advertisements surrounded it? Where was it in the newspaper, let alone the chronological context of the way that particular newspaper reported the same topic over time? Lara Putnam calls this act of jumping in 'side-glancing' and contrasts it with the benefits of travelling to an archive to work through a set of documents:

> Working with tax data or police correspondence in a national archive forced you to read through lots of evidence of political struggle and state formation even when what you really wanted to get at was grain prices or prostitution.[43]

This point is well made, but it is not clear that side-glancing is unique to or inherent in digital texts. In the nineteenth century, the Public Record Office in London began to compile an extensive series of finding aids to the manuscripts of British state papers, largely within its own holdings. These *Calendars of State Papers* not only organised documents on a subject chronologically (which is not necessarily their archival order), but the print volumes included indexes. This print finding aid, one of many, precisely enabled the researcher to swoop into a particular set of documents and, if they chose, cherry-pick without context in just the way that keyword searching allows. Is this not side-glancing?

Indeed, Ann Blair has documented the way that even before the advent of printing, scholars were able to take advantage of a panoply of finding aids that allowed them to avoid actually reading the texts they cited: 'many of the features of the printed reference book ... were adapted to print from medieval manuscript practices' and 'could substitute for reading or rereading'. Often these aids were unacknowledged, along with amanuenses, including wives and children, in just the same way that digital finding aids are often unacknowledged today and research assistants sometimes are too.[44]

This emphatically does not mean that these sceptics are arguing against using digital resources, any more than Blair is arguing against aids such as dictionaries, concordances or catalogues. Putnam herself is clear that the two approaches need to work together:

> We need to complement side-glancing with settling in: taking time to learn about the fullness of what was going on in particular times and places, not just the fragments surfaced among search results.[45]

If we can agree that search is a means and not an end, a technique rather than a methodology, it is still essential that we know as much as possible about what search does in any particular context. Many web users are not aware of how closely Google tailors what it knows about a particular user to the search results presented to them and them alone. At a minimum, Google knows your device, your location, your search history on that device and which results you clicked on previously. If you are logged in to Google it knows much more with certainty. Google is less like a magician and more like a private detective who has read your post and been through your bins. Google is successful precisely because it does this energetically.[46] You can see what more general, untailored results look like by replicating keywords with a search engine like DuckDuckGo, which treats search and searchers as anonymous.[47]

The carry-over effect from the dominance of Google is that we may expect other search engines to act like Google. The effectiveness of Google's single search box may encourage historians to search other resources in the same way, even though such resources cannot work like a Google search because they do not have Google's body of external knowledge.

A fundamental distinction in search results is between *precision* and *recall*. Better precision means that more of the results returned to you are relevant to your query. Better recall means more of the results from the searched documents are returned. Normally, better recall means worse precision, and vice versa. To see this, imagine you are bad at recognising faces. You are at a large party which some people you know will also be attending. If you say hello only to the people you definitely recognise you will have good precision but, because you will ignore some genuine acquaintances, bad recall. If you say hello to anyone vaguely familiar you will have better recall but, because you will greet some strangers like you know them, low precision.

The import of this is that when resources configure their search software, they cannot know your preference for precision or recall, and for you yourself that may vary from case to case anyway. If you have too many results, you will prefer precision to winnow the harvest; if you have too few, you will prefer recall. There are always trade-offs: for the search configuration and for you, when deciding that you have looked through enough results, or that you have tried hard enough to catch everything.

Tim Hitchcock makes a powerful point when he laments that search, and its complexities, is almost entirely absent from the methodology and even professional competence of historians. Not only that, but some search is inherently not reproducible.[48] These are important issues and historians must educate themselves about them and discuss their use of search, and the reading that ensues from it, more openly.

WRITING

Sometimes older technology persists because it has a psychological power, such as the horse-drawn carriage at a funeral.[49] We might suspect the same is true of the academic monograph. In an essay written in 1999, Edward L. Ayers notes that, 'As rapid as the changes have been, however, the actual writing of history has remained virtually untouched and unchanged'.[50] In 2013, writing of the digital, Tim Hitchcock says that 'these developments seem to have little real impact on the kinds of history we write'.[51]

The exciting future of history writing envisaged by Ayers, and by Robert Darnton's proposal of 1999 that the monograph of the future be a many-tiered structure, has largely not been realised at the level of the monograph.[52] The move towards open-access publishing, which we will return to in chapters 2 and 7, for both journal articles and monographs, has made access easier and, if open peer review is also used, more transparent, but it is hard to see that history writing for formal publication has really changed.

Other stages of the writing process have undoubtedly been transformed. The ease with which it is now possible to photograph documents in an archive means that archival visits are sometimes more a corpus-creation exercise. The onsite reading, transcription and note-taking, which require careful thinking about selection, have become less important.[53] A number of studies have suggested that note-taking by hand is more effective for learning, partly because a laptop offers many distractions but partly because, it is thought, writing by hand is slower and therefore requires material to be summarised and consequently processed differently by the brain.[54]

As we discuss in Chapter 6, written outputs for history have proliferated in the internet age. You can, if you choose, write up some preliminary work as a blog or Facebook post and invite comments from other historians. You can tweet asking for advice on a particular theme or source. On average, historians are writing more and for different audiences. Although some think that historians may now begin to write too early in the research process,[55] there are advantages to practising the skill of writing by writing more and more widely. Further, the ease with which text can now be rewritten means historians can more radically revise and reorder work that in a manuscript or typescript format would be prohibitively time-consuming. The previously sharp distinction between periods of research and writing up has faded for technological reasons.

A final dimension in which digital tools change writing is in the new opportunities afforded for collaboration. At the most basic level this might simply involve editing a Google Doc collaboratively with a colleague while talking through the changes via Skype. In this book we will introduce the use of *Git*, which is a free version-control tool that historians can use to collaborate on a text remotely. As usual, however, the choice of tools is enormous.

These are all useful additions to the telephone, the fax machine or the word processor that historians might have previously used to similar effect. But now that historical data is available at scale in machine-readable form, possibilities arise for collaboration with researchers from other disciplines, such as computer scientists or statisticians. When thinking of collaboration across disciplines, it is vital to remember that potential collaborators are unlikely to be interested simply in helping you answer your own research questions. Collaborators are not merely enablers but must have intellectual interests of their own in the work. The level of appeal of our research questions can be hard for historians to gauge because problems that may seem tricky to us might well be blandly uninteresting to an expert from another domain. Nevertheless, messy historical questions can often be interesting, for example, for computer science applications.

One example of such a productive interdisciplinary partnership is the work of Sheryllynne Haggerty, a historian of eighteenth-century British trade, and John Haggerty, a computer scientist. Among other work, they have brought together their respective expertise in the business history of Liverpool and network theory to visualise networks of Liverpool merchants. They were able to analyse 210,000 relationships among 1,700 actors between 1750 and 1810, and show change over time. Their resulting analysis helps to explain the curiosity that, in a city heavily involved in the slave trade, an abolitionist MP was elected in 1806, nominated and seconded by two slave traders. (They suggest that such people had a diverse portfolio and slave trading was not actually central to it in most cases.)[56] For collaborations such as this to be successful, each party must respect the skills and experience of the others but also try to manage the fact that, quite legitimately, the research interests of each party have a different focus and therefore, each party will also have different ideas about where to publish. For an example of this working well, and of what they call 'radical collaboration', we refer you to the Living with Machines project.[57]

CITATION

A less-discussed change to historical method is citation. This development has largely been invisible precisely because the results have been invisible: citation practice largely continues as if we lived in a print-only culture. Not only do many historians silently alter their online reading to print editions, some of them strongly advocate this practice.

The reasons given for choosing obfuscation over transparency are varied but tend to cover three main concerns: that digital links are not permanent; that digital links are not human-readable (because a database reference may be unintelligible); and that URLs are hard to typeset and generally ugly. Usually unspoken is the underlying belief that print citation is more 'scholarly'. As mentioned above, prestige tends to attach to older forms of technology.[58]

To respond to just the first point: print citation itself is not permanent. The survival rate of early modern books has been estimated at 1%.[59] Anyone who thinks that books are natural survivors is invited to leave their personal library in a field for ten years and see what is left upon their return. Books and manuscripts survive so well because a large international infrastructure takes a great deal of care and effort to preserve them. We should all be grateful to librarians and archivists for their expertise, but no comparable infrastructure yet exists for digital objects. In other words, this is a cultural choice we are making, and non-citation of digital undermines the case that digital objects need preserving too.

One of the few people to have skewered this distortion of the online research that went into writing buttressed with print citations is Tim Hitchcock:

> By persevering with a series of outdated formats, and resolutely ignoring the proximate nature of the electronic representations we actually consult, the impact of new technology has been subtly downplayed. History as a discipline, largely uninvolved in the production of digital

resources and apparently uninterested in changing how it illustrates its scholarship to accommodate the digital, has put its head in the sand and tried to ignore the whole issue.[60]

Hitchcock, like Putnam above, makes the important point that reading in analogue form is often immersive, while reading directed by keyword search is 'cherry-picked'. Both types of reading have their place but it is a serious misrepresentation to claim one while doing the other. Ironically, it is often champions of traditional print reading who advocate altering citations, hiding, as it were, a laptop inside a hollowed-out book. The second point Hitchcock emphasises is one we have already mentioned: that the results of online keyword searching are inherently not replicable because of the way that search is individualised and the way that it changes from moment to moment.[61] Citation in such cases should be done with care and honesty.

As historians increasingly use digital resources in preference to analogue ones, their work becomes skewed towards the digital and the digitised. This may be inevitable, just as articles in prestigious journals are more likely to be read and cited than equally good ones in lesser known journals. But to cite only the analogue versions of those sources buries the bias and makes it very hard for readers to recognise and confront it. Ian Milligan exposed the hidden preponderance of digital sources by studying the relative print citation of Canadian newspapers. In Canadian history dissertations, he found, digitised newspapers such as *The Toronto Star* and *Globe and Mail* were an order of magnitude more likely to be cited *as print sources* than the then non-digitised *Montreal Gazette* and *Toronto Telegram*. The discrepancy was not present before the two digitised newspapers were available. 'For the most part', Milligan comments understatedly, the use of online databases in these dissertations 'remains at best implicit'.[62] Doubtless many similar biases in historians' use of sources could be uncovered, but the question is whether they should have been covered up in the first place.

Citation of digital sources does represent a challenge to historians, but it is one we need to confront honestly and not try harder to wish away the more that our real research habits change. Yet again we would point out that there never actually was a golden age of citation that, as Anthony Grafton richly illustrates in his book on the history of the footnote, existed in a state of scholarly perfection. Citation varies across countries, cultures and periods. It often functions less as a pathway for following the researcher's footsteps than of displaying their credentials, which 'perform the function of guild membership or personal recommendation: they give legitimacy'.[63]

CONCLUSION

Historical practice has always been shaped by the availability of evidence and technological affordance, as well as by technical competence, the interests of individuals and the societies they live in, and manifold ideological commitments. Digital history puts these into strong relief. If historical data is freely available in tractable, machine-readable form then it is more likely to be used than if not; what we choose to digitise reveals what we consider most important. In economic terms it is a 'revealed preference', where the value placed on historical information is shown by what people and states will pay for, not by their declarations of interest and support.

Digital, we hope we have made clear, is not a replacement for analogue. Digitisation is not an excuse to destroy the artefact once it has been digitised. Anthony Grafton refers to a scholar in an archive methodically sniffing letters to test for the smell of vinegar, because vinegar was used as a defence against cholera and so the smell could indicate and date a cholera outbreak.[64] The original documents do indeed remain vital for many purposes. Equally vividly, Meg Twycross gives a case study of the kind of manuscript work that can be done with high-quality colour digital images, allowing 'manuscript restoration ... far more effective than anything that was possible before digitization'.[65] Both approaches are needed.

NOTES

1 'C'est une tâche difficile – condamnée à l'avance – que de dire en quelques mots ce qui a vraiment changé dans le domaine de nos études, et surtout comment et pourquoi le changement s'est opéré.' Braudel, *Écrits sur l'histoire*, p. 19.
2 For the effect on doctors, see Gawande, 'Why doctors hate their computers'.
3 Carr, *The Shallows*; Crawford, *The World Beyond Your Head*; Newport, *Digital Minimalism*. Clinical research on digital versus analogue reading is still preliminary, but for a discussion of the issues see Wolf, *Reader, Come Home*.

4 See Gold and Klein, *Debates in the Digital Humanities 2016*, for some of the debates.
5 See the exchange between Winters and Anderson in Tamm and Burke, eds, *Debating New Approaches to History*, especially pp. 291–295.
6 For a contrary view which emphasises the importance of computational thought, see Berry, *The Philosophy of Software*.
7 The project began in the 1930s as a conservation measure: the items were photographed by the company University Microfilms and sold as a microfilm product to research libraries. In the internet age the company, now called ProQuest and merged with another microfilm publisher, Chadwyck-Healey, sold an updated version of the same product via the web, alongside catalogue searching for the many thousands of books available. An offshoot was EEBO-TCP, a project run by a consortium of universities to transcribe fifty thousand of the EEBO page scans in full.
8 Siefring and Meyer, 'Sustaining the EEBO-TCP Corpus in Transition', p. 25.
9 Pons, *El desorden digital*, p. 38.
10 Rockwell and Sinclair, 'Thinking-through the history of computer-assisted textual analysis', in Crompton *et al.*, eds, *Doing Digital Humanities*.
11 Spence, 'Playfair, William (1759–1823)'.
12 Rockwell and Sinclair, 'Thinking-through the history of computer-assisted textual analysis'. A Jupyter notebook (https://jupyter.org/) is an interactive coding environment that runs in a browser, where the results of that code can also be displayed; it was first developed for the Python language, hence the 'py' spelling, but has since been extended to other languages. The Rockwell and Sinclair notebook is available at https://github.com/sgsinclair/epistemologica/blob/master/Mendenhall-CharacteristicCurve.ipynb (both accessed 8 July 2020).
13 'Josephine Miles', Wikipedia, https://en.wikipedia.org/wiki/Josephine_Miles (accessed 8 July 2020).
14 Montgomery *et al.*, eds, *Concordance to the Poetical Works of John Dryden*, introduction, no pagination.
15 Busa *et al.*, *Index Thomisticus*, www.corpusthomisticum.org/it/index.age (accessed 8 July 2020).
16 Conrad and Meyer, 'The economics of slavery in the antebellum South', in the same authors' *The Economics of Slavery*, p. 44.
17 'l'énormité de la documentation semble avoir paralysé les chercheurs', Le Roy Ladurie, 'Le mouvement des loyers parisiens de la fin du Moyen Age au XVIIIe siècle', p. 116 in *Le territoire de l'historien*; 'les techniques modernes ... permettent une véritable révolution historiographique', p. 117.

18 'Professor Sir Roderick Floud', interview transcript, *Making History*, https://archives.history.ac.uk/makinghistory/resources/interviews/Floud_Roderick.html (accessed 8 July 2020).
19 Examples of these criticisms by French and Anglophone historians are summarised in Pons, *El desorden digital*, pp. 53–60.
20 Programma 101, a programmable version of the electronic calculator, was launched in 1964; see 'Programma 101', Wikipedia, https://en.wikipedia.org/wiki/Programma_101 (accessed 8 July 2020).
21 *History and Computing*, 1:1 (1989), iv.
22 *The Programming Historian*, https://programminghistorian.org/ (accessed 8 July 2020).
23 Sassone, 'Survey finds low office productivity linked to staffing imbalances'.
24 Paul Stanley, response to jlconlin, 'Why are default LaTeX margins so big?', *TeX-LaTeX Stack Exchange* (posted 11 September 2012), https://tex.stackexchange.com/questions/71172/why-are-default-latex-margins-so-big#71211 (accessed 8 July 2020).
25 Levy, 'A spreadsheet way of knowledge', originally written in 1984, makes some good points about the cultural changes wrought by the introduction of electronic spreadsheets. For a study of the way in which the use of spreadsheet programs affects how data is used, see Dourish, *The Stuff of Bits*, pp. 81–105. On Microsoft Word, see Berry and Fagerjord, *Digital Humanities*, pp. 92–93.
26 'Las hemos interiorizado como recursos habituales, como si las hubiéran disfrutado desde siempre, como si fueran naturales y no hubieran modificado en absoluto nuestra manera de ejercer la profesión.' Pons, *El desorden digital*, p. 67.
27 This was mentioned in many papers at the 'Negotiating Networks' conference, held in June 2018: https://negotiatingnetworksblog.wordpress.com/ (accessed 8 July 2020).
28 See, for example, Bodard, 'Scanning and printing a Greek vase'.
29 Valerie Johnson cites estimates that the global number of records increased by 60% just in the period from 2013 to the end of 2015. Thomas *et al.*, *The Silence of the Archive*, p. 74.
30 D'Ignazio and Klein, *Data Feminism*, p. 151.
31 Osterberg, 'Update on the Twitter archive at the Library of Congress'.
32 Schafer *et al.*, 'Paris and Nice terrorist attacks: Exploring Twitter and web archives'.
33 The Internet Archive Wayback Machine, https://archive.org/web/web.php (accessed 8 July 2020).
34 The British Library's UK Web Archive be found at www.bl.uk/collection-guides/uk-web-archive (accessed 8 July 2020).

35 UK Web Archive, www.webarchive.org.uk/ukwa/ (accessed 8 July 2020).
36 Brügger and Schroeder, *The Web as History*.
37 Cowls, 'Cultures of the UK web', in Brügger and Schroeder, eds, *The Web as History*.
38 Bush, 'As we may think'.
39 Licklider, *Libraries of the Future*.
40 Hitchcock, 'Digital affordances for criminal justice history'.
41 *Dictionary of National Biography on CD-ROM*, insert booklet.
42 Cohen, 'From Babel to knowledge'.
43 Putnam, 'The transnational and the text-searchable'.
44 Blair, *Too Much to Know*, p. 7.
45 Putnam, 'The transnational and the text-searchable', 401.
46 Zuboff, *The Age of Surveillance Capitalism*.
47 DuckDuckGo, https://duckduckgo.com (accessed 8 July 2020).
48 Hitchcock, 'Confronting the digital', 14–16.
49 Edgerton, *The Shock of the Old*, p. 11; Raulff, *Farewell to the Horse*, pp. 1–46.
50 Ayers, 'The pasts and futures of digital history'.
51 Hitchcock, 'Confronting the digital', 11.
52 Darnton, 'A program for reviving the monograph'.
53 Pons, *El desorden digital*, p. 205.
54 'Attention, students: put your laptops away', *NPR Weekend Edition Sunday* (17 April 2016), www.npr.org/2016/04/17/474525392/attention-students-put-your-laptops-away (accessed 8 July 2020).
55 Grafton, *Worlds Made by Words*, p. 315.
56 Haggerty and Haggerty, 'The life cycle of a metropolitan business network'.
57 Living with Machines, http://livingwithmachines.ac.uk/ (accessed 8 July 2020).
58 Blaney and Siefring, 'A culture of non-citation'.
59 Ann Blair, 'Afterword', p. 315 in Corens, Peters and Walsham, eds, *Archives and Information in the Early Modern World*.
60 Hitchcock, 'Confronting the digital', 12.
61 Hitchcock, 'Confronting the digital', 14–16.
62 Milligan, 'Illusionary order', 565.
63 Grafton, *The Footnote: A Curious History*, p. 7. For an example of social change affecting citation practice, see also Veyne, *Les grecs, ont-ils cru à leurs mythes?*, pp. 17–24.
64 Grafton, *Worlds Made by Words*, p. 311, quoting Brown and Duguid, *The Social Life of Information*, pp. 173–174.
65 Twycross, 'Virtual restoration and manuscript archaeology', in Greengrass and Hughes, eds, *The Virtual Representation of the Past*, p. 26.

2

FORMULATING YOUR RESEARCH QUESTIONS

INTRODUCTION

This book is concerned with digital history, and that necessarily means working with primary sources that are available in digital form. 'Digital', however, encompasses a large and diverse range of materials. The most obvious distinction the historian faces is that between sources which have been digitised from a physical original, for example a thirteenth-century manuscript or a nineteenth-century newspaper, and sources which are described as 'born digital', such as emails, Word documents or web pages. Once your source is available in machine-readable form, most of the methods described in this book will be applicable, regardless of whether it began life as writing on parchment or as binary code. But before you get started with your research, it is vital to understand the way in which your digital source was created, and how it has been made available to you. The growing interest in material culture has led, among other things, to a much greater focus on the ways in which books and newspapers were produced, circulated and used. Historians working with digital sources need to have the same understanding of how their sources have been created and how platforms, interfaces and editorial choices affect the kinds of analysis that can be undertaken.

This chapter will explore the different ways in which historical documents of all kinds are digitised and how much you need to know about these processes in order to use digital materials effectively in your research. It will also explore why certain primary sources are digitised rather than others, and what kinds of gaps and omissions you should be looking for. It will discuss the value of open data, and the different kinds of analysis that are possible when you have direct access to machine-readable text (in many different formats) rather than being constrained (or guided) by a search engine or platform. It will consider the differences between digitised primary sources and primary sources that have always taken digital form, and briefly discuss the differences between text, data and metadata. It will conclude with some suggestions about what we hope will be your final goal: publication of some kind. Digital projects come in all sizes and we would urge you to write up and share with others what you have found, even in a small project. Publication might not be your only goal but we suggest you keep it in mind as one of your goals, even at the very beginning of your research.

WHAT DIGITAL SOURCES WILL I FIND?

Most historians are still likely to be working primarily with digitised rather than born-digital sources. Historians of the twentieth century have been the least well served by the mass digitisation that has taken place since the advent of the World Wide Web. The large-scale digitisation of newspapers has transformed how we study the eighteenth and nineteenth centuries, but copyright restrictions mean that most newspaper databases only cover the period up to about 1900.[1] For some collections, an even more risk-averse approach is adopted. The British Library's Heritage Made Digital programme, for example, is 'sticking to a 140-year rule – so the run of the newspaper has to have ended by 1878'.[2] In this case, whole newspaper runs will have been excluded from the digitisation process even though most of the material is out of copyright. Primary sources of a later date, including sound and moving image, are likely to have even more restrictive access conditions, to be published as part of expensive commercial packages or simply not to be available at all.

There are other inequalities of digitisation and access too, beyond the constraints of time period and intellectual property rights. As Lara Putnam notes: 'the universe of digitized text is anything but representative of the temporal and geographic contours of human life in the past. The nineteenth- and early-twentieth-century Anglophone world has been ground zero of digitization.'[3] For all places and periods, the totality of primary sources will never be digitised, but for the medieval or early modern historian the amount that is available makes it possible to work largely with digital materials.

DIGITISATION CAN TRANSFORM RESEARCH: THE EXAMPLE OF HANSARD

Historical research is not 'data-driven', nor is it determined by technology. But it is shaped by the sources that exist, the form in which they are available and the ease with which they may be accessed. Take Hansard, for example, which is the more-or-less verbatim record of proceedings in the UK Parliament.[4] The first volume of *Cobbett's Parliamentary Debates* (which came to be known by the name of publisher Thomas Curson Hansard) was published in 1804, covering the period from 22 November 1803 to 29 March 1804.[5] Since then, more than three thousand printed volumes have been published, serving as an invaluable source for the study of Parliament, politics and society over two centuries. Hansard has always allowed historians to explore the political careers of individuals, to study particular parliaments or even governments, to understand the establishment and development of political parties, and to consider important events as they were discussed in the Lords and the Commons. Browsing and reading were assisted by 'extensive tables of contents, and person and subject indices, while composite index volumes were sometimes published'.[6] It could be used like any work of reference, but nobody would ever have attempted to read it from cover to cover. Then in 2008, a pilot project was launched to digitise and publish online all volumes of Hansard to 2004, more than three million pages.[7] Not only was the full text of Hansard published online as XML files, but a decision was taken to make those files openly available and downloadable.[8] We will cover working with XML in Chapter 5.

Historians and other humanities researchers were quick to take advantage of digital Hansard, and a number of new research projects were funded to exploit the potential of this rich dataset. The online interface developed by the parliamentary team was fairly rudimentary, but the openness of the data meant that researchers could download it, manipulate and enhance it, and then make the enhanced data available for reuse and further development by others. The Parliamentary Discourse project opened up Hansard for linguistic research, producing a corpus from more than 7.5 million texts (by nearly forty thousand individual speakers). This corpus was in turn enhanced by the Samuels project, which tagged all of the words in the corpus contextually for meaning, drawing on the *Historical Thesaurus of English*.[9] The Linking Parliamentary Records through Metadata project created a unified metadata schema which described all of the people, bills, acts, items of business, debates, divisions and sessions mentioned in Hansard, making it possible to find every speech made by a particular MP or to trace the passage of an act through Parliament.[10] This then opened the way for the Digging into Linked Parliamentary Data project, which developed an interface that allowed researchers to search across parliamentary proceedings from Canada, the Netherlands and the UK, and explore terms and concepts associated with particular speakers and parties over time.[11]

This pattern of iteration, of building on previous work to create something that is larger in scale or connected to other digital resources, is common in digital history. In this instance, the decision to digitise Hansard initiated a series of projects which draw on and connect to each other, collectively changing what it is possible to know about parliamentary debate and discourse in modern Britain.

The ripples do not stop there. As Hansard began to be published online routinely, allowing anyone 'to see what a Member has said within three hours of them saying it', it became possible to bring together the historical and contemporary material on a platform that is much more user-friendly than the interface for the first digitised Hansard.[12] People can search the full text of Hansard, browse sittings, and find divisions, debates and MPs. This new platform is much easier for researchers to use than the separate interface for the historical content, which still exists online, and requires no experience of working with XML. It does, however, constrain what you are able to do, and does not support the kind of linkage and experimentation that is possible when you can download and manipulate data directly.

Most people's experience of working with digital data will be through a platform like Hansard Online. It delivers immediately relevant results, but at the cost of control and, inevitably, some insight. It is not always easy to understand precisely what it is you are searching or browsing, and how the choices made by editors, technical developers and other project staff are predetermining what you might be able to find.

It is to the credit of the team behind Hansard Online that they have highlighted one of the key things that historians should be aware of when using the database: it combines digitised and born-digital data. This directly affects the quality, and even type, of results that you will find if you enter keywords into the deceptively simple search box. The contemporary Hansard text is born digital, created specifically for publication online. It has specially created metadata which allows you, for example, to search for and collate all of the information for an individual

MP. Not only is this metadata not present for the historical material, but the way in which that material was digitised means that search results will not be as accurate or comprehensive as they would be for the later content. The 'About' page for the website also notes: 'We are aware that a small number of volumes for both Houses are missing ... If you are looking for content from between 2005 and 2006, you may be able to access this through a legacy site.'[13] This is vital context of which many users will never be aware because they launch straight into conducting a keyword search and never venture near explanatory material. When working with Hansard or any digital source, understanding the parameters and limitations of that source is crucial.

WHAT DOES 'DIGITISED' MEAN?

When thinking about how you are going to use digital sources in your research, it is not enough simply to know that something has been digitised. What this means will vary widely between and even within online resources. Choices around what is digitised, and how, are often directly associated with budget and cost. The easiest and cheapest method is simply to produce a digital facsimile of a manuscript, book or newspaper, consisting of scanned images of folios or pages. This is the model adopted by the Anglo-American Legal Tradition website, which as of August 2015 had published online 9.25 million 'frames' of legal documents held in the National Archives of the UK (TNA), spanning the reigns of Richard I (1189–99) and Victoria (1837–1901).[14] The benefits of being able to access these digitised documents from anywhere in the world cannot be overstated, but the mode of engagement is little changed from working with the physical manuscripts in a TNA reading room. It is not possible to search the documents, and navigation is by thumbnail image, structured according to the archival record series. The quality of the images is variable, but a degree of magnification (zooming) is both possible and useful. The novelty is to be able to close read a manuscript located in an archive in London from your own room in Durham, New York or Tokyo.

A resource like the Anglo-American Legal Tradition can be accessed and used most successfully by someone who already has detailed knowledge of the physical manuscripts and how they have been catalogued. No sophisticated digital skills are required, but no real overview of the material is possible. This places limitations on the kinds of research that can be undertaken. These limitations begin to be overcome when digitisation results in the production of text that is not just human-readable but also machine-readable, thereby unlocking search and other forms of quantitative analysis.

There are several different ways of generating this machine-readable text, and again the choices made will affect how you can use a particular database, even if this is not immediately obvious. In the next chapter we will discuss the differences between text that has been generated using optical character recognition (OCR) and text that has been rekeyed, and will emphasise that the latter will be much more accurate than the former. It can, however, be very hard to judge just how many errors may be present in the text that you are searching, which more often than not will be hidden behind a beautiful facsimile image.

Detailed information is very hard to come by, but in some instances a resource will not just mention the method of digitisation that has been used, but even provide statistics that will help you to evaluate what you are searching. British History Online, for example, notes that its texts have been digitised by double-rekeying, which 'involves two typists inputting text independently from page scans. The two transcriptions are then compared and any differences are manually resolved.' This has resulted in text which is at least 99.995% accurate when compared to the original – that is to say, only one character in every twenty thousand will have been wrongly transcribed.

The majority of digital resources may reveal that OCR has been used, but will usually give no more information than that. Often, and particularly with more mature digital resources, the methods of digitisation were simply not documented in sufficient detail at the time. Subsequent research is frequently needed to reveal the limitations of a dataset. In 2009, for example, Tanner *et al.* demonstrated that material digitised for the British Library's nineteenth-century newspapers project had a character accuracy rate of 83.6%, a word accuracy rate of 78% and an accuracy rate of 63.4% for words beginning with a capital letter. In other words, 16.4 out of every 100 characters was rendered wrongly and 22 out of every 100 words contained a mistake. The situation was even worse for the personal and place names that historians are often most interested in looking for – 36.6 out of every 100 such words contained errors and thus would be hard to discover through search.[15]

It is worth considering that the accuracy of OCR may not even be consistent within a single dataset, significantly affecting your ability to, for example, compare the frequency of particular names, words or phrases over time. This is very likely to be true for digital resources which have been added to over a period of years, or which have been developed in stages. OCR technology has improved enormously since it first began to be used, and in general the older the digital resource, the more likely it is that there will be a lower degree of accuracy. Similarly, 'The older the newspaper, the lower the accuracy rate is likely to be, and accuracy rates are generally lower for newspapers than for books and journals'.[16] The OCRed text may have been generated from the scanned pages of a book, pamphlet or newspaper, or there may have been an intermediate microfilm stage, or both of these methods may have been used in combination. All of these production decisions will affect what you will be able to do, and what you will be able to find when you search a digital resource.

Another factor to consider is the scope or comprehensiveness of a digital resource. How representative is this particular set of newspapers, books or manuscripts? Is it easy to discover what has been included or excluded, and why? The Old Bailey Proceedings Online states clearly that it is making available 'a fully searchable, digitised collection of all surviving editions of the Old Bailey Proceedings from 1674 to 1913, and of the Ordinary of Newgate's Accounts between 1676 and 1772'.[17] If you are interested in the records of the Old Bailey, you need look no further. In contrast, why has British History Online only digitised volumes 4, 5 (part 1), 6 (part 1), 7 (part 1), 10 (part 1) and 11 of the Staffordshire Historical Collection?[18] The British Library Newspapers collection contains 'the most comprehensive collection of national and regional newspapers of Victorian Britain available'.[19] The more recent Heritage Made Digital programme at the British Library uses different criteria. It is concerned with 'digitising parts of our collection that have never been made available online before, or are underrepresented in our online collections'.[20] In a blog post about the programme, it is revealed that other factors that have been taken into consideration: 'we have chosen to concentrate on newspapers in a poor or unfit condition'; 'We are only digitising newspapers that are out of copyright'; 'we are primarily digitising newspapers that [were] published in London but which were distributed outside London as well'.[21] Decisions of this kind have to be made – there is neither the time nor the money for cultural heritage institutions to digitise all of their holdings – but, like all curatorial choices, they will determine what historians have access to now and in the future. As the same blog post points out: 'It's worth remembering that the British Library has 60 million newspapers, from 1619 to the present day. After a decade or more of intensive work, we have digitised just 5%. There is a long, long way to go.'[22]

So far, we have been thinking mainly about the digitisation of printed materials dating from the eighteenth century or later. But what if your research concerns medieval manuscripts, early printed books, handwritten scientific papers from the seventeenth-century or nineteenth-century correspondence? If OCR can generate high error rates when dealing with print, what are the options for digitising and then working with other kinds of primary source? Until the rapid improvement in handwriting recognition technology, the only option available would have been laborious and time-consuming manual transcription. Many historians will have found themselves in the position of having to digitise their own sources, most likely using a standard word-processing package. This is largely unseen work, which supports individual research, but rarely becomes available for others to use. Another, now commonplace method of digitisation is the taking of photographs in libraries and archives, usually with a mobile phone. If you know the material you are interested in using, it makes much more sense to spend a few days in an archive taking photographs of membranes and folios than to spend weeks or months in a reading room transcribing text. This shift in historical practice has led to the development of tools like Tropy, which allows you to organise and document your research photos, and 'shortens the path from finding archival sources to writing about them'.[23]

Some digital projects have employed small teams of researchers to undertake this work of imaging and high-quality manual transcription and/or translation, particularly where the body of primary sources is relatively limited in size. The Henry III Fine Rolls Project is a good example of this approach.[24] The fine rolls are part of the financial records of the medieval English state, recording promised payments to the crown in return for a wide range of rights, including those involving marriage and property. Indexing of the fine rolls was possible because the scope of the project was limited to the reign of a single king, covering the years 1216–72. Thanks to this project, historians can now undertake much more detailed analysis and ask different questions of this period than they can for the reign of other medieval monarchs. However, the limitations are obvious; for instance, it is possible to trace connections between people mentioned in this subset of the fine rolls, but not how those connections might have extended beyond 1272. That would require a larger longitudinal dataset to have been translated and prepared in a similar way. The work of a small group of researchers, often funded for a limited period of time, does not scale up.

It is this problem of scale that lies behind newer methods of digitising pre-modern or non-print sources. In the first decade of the twenty-first century, the interactive technologies and behaviours that characterise Web 2.0 began to be exploited by academic researchers and memory institutions to expand the number and type of people who could help with the digitisation of cultural heritage materials. Crowdsourcing entered our vocabulary.[25]

The authors of *Academic Crowdsourcing in the Humanities*, Stuart Dunn and Mark Hedges, have developed a typology of crowdsourcing as it has been used in the academic humanities, organised into four facets: asset type, process type, task type and output type. Their understanding is that 'A *process* is a sequence of *tasks* ... through which an *output* is produced by operating on an *asset*' (original emphasis). The processes they identify include a wide range of actions, including collaborative tagging, linking, mapping, translating and categorising, but there is no doubt that it is transcription which has been most widely used in digitisation.[26] Sometimes, transcription involves the correction of text which has already been generated using OCR. Some of the problems associated with OCRing newspapers that we identified above were tackled in this way by the Trove Newspapers project at the National Library of Australia.[27] The OCR was presented alongside the page image and users were encouraged to correct typos, add in missing text and so on. In addition to resulting in a much more accurate corpus of text for historians to study, this shed light on the digitisation process itself. Users could see, for example, that italicised type tended to have a higher error rate than normal type, or that hyphenation at the end of lines might cause problems. This knowledge is enormously valuable when considering what to look out for when searching text that is hidden behind the interface. The idea of co-creation, of people working together to make digitised primary sources more susceptible to analysis, is clearly acknowledged on the Trove website: 'Trove is yours. As you text correct, comment, tag or contribute content you are helping to build a better service for everyone.'[28]

Many other projects have employed crowdsourcing methods to turn digital facsimiles into searchable text. The New York Public Library, for example, used this method to produce transcriptions of its collection of historical restaurant menus. At the time of writing, more than 1.3 million dishes have been transcribed, from more than 17,500 menus,

FORMULATING YOUR RESEARCH QUESTIONS 35

creating an enormously valuable resource for historians of food, culture and consumption.[29] The National Archives of the UK and the Imperial War Museum collaborated with the crowdsourcing platform Zooniverse on Operation War Diary to engage volunteers in transcribing and annotating First World War field notes from the Western Front.[30]

Libraries and archives have often taken the lead on initiatives of this kind, as they seek to open up their collections to wider and different audiences, but research projects based in universities have also employed co-creation as a means of digitising historical documents. One of the earliest, launched in 2010, was the Transcribe Bentham project at University College London. To date, more than twenty thousand pages of Bentham's collected papers have been transcribed, representing almost half of the total collection.

The Transcribe Bentham project is directly linked to another enormously promising digitisation initiative, READ (which stands for Recognition and Enhancement of Archival Documents).[31] This project has the potential to bring about the digitisation of complex handwritten material at a scale that would previously have been beyond the scope of quantitative digital analysis. Bentham's papers were among those digitised primary sources used to test and develop handwritten text recognition (HTR) technology used by the project. The digitised images of Bentham's letters and papers, together with the crowdsourced transcriptions, were used as training data by the Transkribus platform.[32] The results were so successful that the platform can be used 'to recognise Bentham's hand with an average Character Error Rate of just 9% (meaning that 91% of characters are transcribed correctly by the machine)'.[33] If you remember our earlier discussion of OCR, this is a lower error rate than achieved for the British Library Newspapers project. To achieve this degree of accuracy in transcription was not a quick or easy process, and the *neural networks* used in HTR had to be trained and re-trained over time, with human intervention required to identify where and why things were going wrong. However, the technology is improving all the time. It is likely that HTR technology will follow broadly the same path as OCR technology, developing gradually and proving more suitable for some kinds of handwriting and handwritten documents than others, but it is already transforming the ways in which previously inaccessible primary sources can be used. If the comparison with OCR is accurate, however, very soon historians will be facing the same issues of hidden accuracy rates, differential results for material digitised at different times, and constraints arising from the decision made about which collections to prioritise for this kind of digitisation. In the meantime, 'Anyone can start a test project in Transkribus by uploading around 75 pages of digitised images to the platform and transcribing each page as fully as possible'.[34]

If the sources that you want to work with are unlikely to be digitised by someone else, why not try digitising it yourself, and in the process change the kind of research that you are able to do?

ACCESS TO DIGITAL DATA

Not all digital data is created equal, and there are similar inequalities when it comes to gaining access to digitised and born-digital primary sources. Assuming that the material you want to work with is available in digital form, you will generally be able to explore it by means of an interface which allows you to search and/or browse. We have already discussed the single search box which characterises so many digital resources, but there will often be more sophisticated filtering and search options that you can use. Let us look at the Old Bailey Online. The default option for users on the home page is to conduct a keyword search. Results can be filtered by specifying whether you want to search across the full digitised dataset, a subset or a particular piece of text (identified by reference number). The dedicated search page, however, allows you to 'combine keyword searches with queries on tagged information including surname, crime, and punishment sentence'.[35] This immediately gives you greater insight both into the nature of the original records and into how information they contain has been *marked up* during the digitisation process (we will discuss markup, and what it means for a text to be marked up, in Chapter 5). An editorial decision has been taken to support search not just by keyword but also according to combinations of particular significant criteria. This offers much more flexibility in your search queries, but the possibilities are not, and cannot be, limitless.

A search interface opens up content to interrogation and exploration, but it also inevitably restricts the kinds of question that you can ask. Those restrictions have been determined by subject experts, but they are restrictions nonetheless. It is for this reason that the team behind the Old Bailey Online have developed an API (application programming interface) which allows you to determine for yourself how you would like to work with the data.[36] Working with the API is not straightforward, even though an API demonstrator and instructions for developers have been made available, but it does give you the option to export subsets of the data so that you can work with them using other tools and methods. The Old Bailey Online is a good example of a digital resource which has been constructed in such a way as to allow access by non-specialist as well as expert users.

At the opposite end of the spectrum are those digital resources which have been created by commercial organisations, sometimes in partnership with libraries and archives. We described the origins of the Ancestry corpus in Chapter 1: it is now one of the largest collections of digitised historical sources available, accessible through its various national websites. The UK platform offers an impressive range of search options, but the platform foregrounds locating individual records rather than conducting longitudinal analysis across the dataset. For a subscription fee, you will be allowed to read and download single records, or groups of records, but as an individual researcher you will not be able to take away data.[37] It is not just commercial platforms that limit access to data in this way, however. British History Online, for example, includes the following guidance for users of the site: 'We ask that you do not produce more than a few lines of content without permission. If you would like to use a larger section of text, please contact us directly. Unfortunately, we cannot guarantee that we will be able to grant permission to reproduce text.'[38] Restrictions of this kind will often be the result of underlying concerns about copyright, but they do shape the kinds of research that you will be able to do.

Many digital projects have worked hard to make their data as open as possible, and you may find that you are able to download information without even having to go through an API. Downloadable data may take several formats, and this will influence how can you use it. The simplest is the comma-separated values (CSV) file, which stores tabular data in 'plain text' form. It is not suitable for unstructured text. CSV files can be opened in standard programmes like Excel or Google Sheets, so you will not need any particular programming skills to get started. You might also be offered the option to download data in JSON (JavaScript Object Notation), which 'is a lightweight data-interchange format. It is easy for humans to read and write. It is easy for machines to parse and generate.'[39] The Historical Hansard website gives a range of download options, which include JSON. It even notes that you can get JSON output for a person simply by adding .js to a person URL.[40] You can easily convert CSV to JSON and vice versa, although be careful when you open files in a programme like Excel as it can introduce errors (we will discuss this in Chapter 7). Many digital projects encode text using XML, which like JSON is both readily human- and machine-readable. Where copyright is not a concern, they may make available the full text of a digital corpus in XML format. On 1 January 2015, the Early English Books Online Text Creation Partnership (EEBO-TCP) published twenty-five thousand transcribed texts under an open licence, not just in XML but also as HTML and ePUB (an ebook format).[41] The files could be downloaded by anyone, either from GitHub or the Oxford University Research Archive.[42] Like most digital history projects that are primarily concerned with text, the XML conforms to an internationally recognised standard, the Text Encoding Initiative (TEI). This means that if you have XML files from different sources, as long as they have been marked up using TEI-XML you will be able to link them and, for example, discover if they contain information about the same people. We discuss these formats, particularly XML, at much greater length in Chapter 5, and show you how you can work with them in complex ways.

You may come across data that uses the Resource Description Framework (RDF). RDF is an abstract data model which is agnostic about how it is expressed as a format (the technical term for this expression is 'serialisation'). This means that you may find RDF data in formats we have already mentioned, particularly XML. RDF divides everything up into 'triples', which are groups of three elements comprising subject, object and predicate. The predicate describes the relationship between subject and object:

```
"Eliza King" residentOf "Balls Pond Road"
```

In itself this does not seem like much. But you can see that if combined with thousands of other triples about Balls Pond Road, or millions of triples about London streets, it could become a powerful source of information, greater than the sum of its parts. RDF is intended to work at scale and requires specialist tools to query, so we suggest you do not start using it lightly for your own data.[43]

Regardless of the format in which data is made available to you, the key point is that there are immediately more options once you can work with it on your own computer, using your own tools. You can experiment and, perhaps even more importantly, you can get things wrong and start again. Finding the right approach is a process of trial and error, and this is much easier if you can try things out on a small

FORMULATING YOUR RESEARCH QUESTIONS 39

sample of data or combine several different tools and methods. You can help other researchers by being open with your data and processes too. For the time being, there is still a lot of historical data which is locked away from more experimental research, but this is likely to improve as openness is encouraged in research and publishing. Copyright exemptions for text and data mining are likely to open up the possibilities for accessing not just newly digitised materials but data that has previously been relatively closed.

USING BORN-DIGITAL SOURCES

Some historians will want to work with born-digital primary sources, especially as we get further away from the advent of email, the web and social media. Document servers rather than printed files will begin to find their way into archives, and there are already examples of what are known as hybrid archives (containing analogue and digital materials) in places like the British Library.[44] Born-digital materials do not present the same challenges as digitised sources in terms of accuracy and searchability, but this does not mean that they are straightforward to use. It is important to understand how born-digital archives have been created before you can use them effectively, and if good documentation is patchy for digitised sources it is almost non-existent for the majority of born-digital collections. This is partly a question of scale. The British Library may hold sixty million newspapers, but the UK Web Archive, also based at the library, collects billions of web pages, images, videos, PDFs and so on every year.[45] This volume of information cannot yet be catalogued or described in any meaningful way, and historians still largely have to fall back on keyword searching and serendipitous qualitative analysis. This has a significant effect on the kinds of research questions that you can ask, as does the inability of most historians to get access to high-performance computing facilities of the kind needed to interrogate terabytes of data.

Decisions about what to digitise are generally taken by people, whether they are expert archivists and librarians or publishers who have spotted a gap in the market, but some large born-digital archives are created almost entirely by algorithms. The UK Web Archive, for example, is the result of 'an automated collection of UK websites (otherwise known as a "crawl") at least once a year'.[46] The crawler program is fed an initial list of URLs which it then works through, finding other links to follow, and so on. The result is a large and messy dataset which will contain many different kinds of media and multiple copies of the same web pages, which the crawler has found through different routes.

Although algorithms have an unfortunate reputation for objectivity, and may also be opaque even to the people who create them, they are not and cannot be value free. Algorithms reflect the goals, assumptions and biases of their producers; they are 'opinions embedded in mathematics'.[47] Digital archives created algorithmically, then, should be interrogated as robustly as any other archive.

Duplication is a feature of many kinds of born-digital sources, and this complicates quantitative analysis significantly. In a sample set of 106 email messages held at the George W. Bush Presidential Library that deal with a single topic – the No Child Left Behind Act (2001) – only 23 contain unique content; the remaining 83 are duplicates.[48] This duplication makes it very challenging to analyse trends over time, as it is not always possible to discern whether you are identifying a historical phenomenon that is worthy of further investigation or simply a dataset that has been distorted by the vagaries of the collection process or by the structure of the underlying technology.

Born-digital archives pose many other difficulties for researchers, including, for example, the fact that they are not fixed: content may suddenly be removed from public access for data protection reasons; or new material may even be added once you have finished your research if its legal status changes or technical restrictions are relaxed. The date on which you consult a primary source becomes newly important when working with born-digital archives. You can only say definitively what information was there when you looked at it, which may sometimes be different for another historian looking at the same archive four months later. New tools and methods for working with large and heterogeneous born-digital archives are emerging all the time, but for the time being they are best approached with caution and a clear-eyed awareness of the challenges and limitations. Born-digital archives hold enormous promise for historical research, and in many instances are rapidly replacing familiar analogue sources; but we are only just beginning to unlock them.[49]

TEXT, DATA AND METADATA

As we have already discussed, most historians will still be working with digital text rather than with sound or the still or moving image. We have used 'text' and 'data' more or less interchangeably here because, thanks to digitisation and the advent of born-digital sources, 'the information encoded in text is a rich complement to the more structured kind of data traditionally used in research'.[50] The data – the text – can be explored and manipulated using the methods outlined in this book, but even where the text itself is inaccessible or not susceptible to easy analysis, metadata can help to structure information and derive meaning. The *OED* defines metadata as 'data whose purpose is to describe and give information about other data',[51] and it is an important means of navigating the digital landscape and of understanding, structuring and sharing data. Every time you create a file on your computer, you are producing metadata, from the name that you choose to give the file to the automatically generated information about time and date, authorship and so on.[52] This helps you to find the file later and, if you name it carefully, to work out what it contains. Information about time and date helps you to look for the most recent version of something, or even understand its versioning history.

Where the data itself cannot be searched, for example in digital resources that only publish facsimile images rather than machine-readable text, metadata can still allow you to find some of what you need. When EEBO was launched in 1998, there was no viable technical option for digitising the text of more than 130,000 works printed in English before 1700.[53] The way it was set up means users can search the bibliographic metadata, including title, author, date, subject keyword and country of origin. This means of access will be familiar to anyone who has used a digital catalogue in a library or archive. In this instance, metadata acts as a means of navigation, discovery and ordering, but in some circumstances it can become the object of study itself. This is the case for the archived web, which is often either inaccessible for copyright reasons or simply too large for historians to work with. Faced with the vastness of the archived web, Ian Milligan argues that 'while our first instinct ... might be to go right to the content, more fruitful historical information can be found within the metadata'.[54] Using the metadata alone, you can study file formats, reconstruct the links and connections between websites, trace the flows of information online. The presence of extensive and/or high-quality metadata can transform the kind of research that is possible, even if the data itself is problematic or closed to public access.

PUBLICATION

At the beginning of any substantial amount of work, whether it is research you are doing on your own or a full-scale funded project, you should establish the means of telling the world about it. This is not pure altruism: you might get advice from people doing similar work, offers of collaboration, or help with a technical problem. For all of these reasons it pays to present your work honestly, and not as a series of triumphs.

If you want to communicate about a project as it proceeds, we recommend that you decide in advance what you are going to do and who will be responsible for what. If you are going to start a Twitter account or a Facebook page, what will be on it and how often do you plan to post? A vague plan that 'we will just share the work between us' might possibly work but a formal schedule is more likely to succeed. Having such a formal schedule makes this sound like hard work. Good. You should be looking at communication of the project as a proper part of the work, and one that takes time, not as an add-on. You can make your posts quite rare if you choose, but they will still sometimes have to be written when you are busy with other things; if they are not in your schedule, they will not get priority.

In our experience, starting something like a Twitter or Instagram account for a specific time-limited project is not a good idea. Once the project is over the accounts will go dormant or have to be deleted and the project becomes hard to contact. A better approach if possible is to use an existing account with a hashtag for your project. An institutional account is ideal for this but a personal account, even if you have to open a new one, would work too. Of course, if you plan to continue with this project for the rest of your working life then its Twitter feed is the least of your commitments and you need have no qualms about starting one.

If you are averse to social media then you may prefer to start a blog for the project (although, of course, you can do both). Tedious though it can be to have to moderate comments, you should have comments enabled. If you choose to pre-moderate or not is up to you, but a blog post followed by lots of spam can make the blog look like the neglected front garden to your project.

Formal publication is usually the final act of a project, but you could also share your methodology as well. If you really run out of time you may think 'I really should write this project up some time' and move on. Try to resist this temptation because this kind of communication is not only an important contribution to historical research in itself but a means of other people discovering your project, learning from it and perhaps using your data for further research. If you are working collaboratively, you should discuss early on in the project what the writing up process is going to be. Who is writing about what, and whose names will be on it? If you are doing the actual writing together you need to decide the order of your names and agree on the process and tools you will all need to use to work together: if one person wants to write in Word and another in LaTeX (much used by researchers in science and the social sciences), that could cause friction. If one person is writing a piece on their own, will the others have a chance to review it before submission to ensure that nothing is, in their view, misrepresented?

You will notice that in terms of formal publication we have assumed that you want to publish a journal article rather than a book chapter. Journal articles are often perceived as having higher academic status than book chapters because the former should be rigorously peer-reviewed and the latter are often not at all.

If your project has a strong digital element then your first choice is whether to publish in a history journal or a digital humanities journal. You can even do both, reserving a focus on the historical findings for a journal specialising in your area and a technical article for a journal with a digital humanities theme. A technical article need not be ground-breaking but does need to contain something of interest in the technical approach for knowledgeable readers. You may not feel able to write this yourself. Frequently, the make-up of the team can dictate where you publish: in interdisciplinary collaborations each member of the team is likely to publish in different places.

We will discuss data repositories (online collections of files) in Chapter 6, along with other advice on how to look after your data. If you have made data publicly available then you should certainly refer to it, even if you publish in the most traditional of print journals; but be aware that this reference creates a duty for you to keep that data available in the stated location for a long time to come. The costs of keeping data public for years emphasise the benefit of an institutional repository, where you may also be required to deposit a copy of the article itself.

If you publish in an online-only journal, especially if it has a technical focus, it may be possible to publish the data (especially if it is small) with the article so that readers can download it directly. This can be discussed with the journal in advance. However, it is unwise to use this as the only route to publication of data.

Some people in digital humanities have an instinctive preference for open-access journals; they want their work to be free to everyone. This is a noble principle, but if you know of a journal that would be perfect for your work that is not open access, we would advise you to submit to it anyway. This is probably the journal that everyone in your field reads. If there are options for your institution to pay for your article to be open access (which is sometimes possible) then all the better.

At the time of writing, Plan S, which mandates open-access publishing across Europe, is being rolled out. The landscape in publishing is changing, and we make some broader predictions about what that will mean in our final chapter; but for journal publishing at least, open access seems as if it will become the dominant model.

CONCLUSION

Whatever data or metadata you want to use as a digital historian, it is essential to understand how it has come into being. How was it created, by whom and why? Finding this out is part of the research process, and it is not always as easy to discover as it should be, particularly for older digital resources which are no longer actively developed. You will almost certainly come across problems and challenges, and most likely discover that you cannot do everything you initially wanted to do. But by exploring an API or working imaginatively with metadata, you will also open up new possibilities. Digital tools and data do not determine what research you will want to do, but their limitations and availability will certainly shape how you do it. Explaining how availability and limitation shaped your work should be part of your published outputs. It is easy to focus on the problems, as this chapter has done to an extent, but that is just a first step to revealing the potential of digital history.

NOTES

1 British Library, Collection Guides: British Newspaper Archive, www.bl.uk/collection-guides/british-newspaper-archive (accessed 5 July 2020).
2 British Library, 'Heritage Made Digital – the newspapers', *The Newsroom*

FORMULATING YOUR RESEARCH QUESTIONS

blog (7 January 2019), blogs.bl.uk/thenewsroom/2019/01/heritage-made-digital-the-newspapers.html (accessed 9 March 2020).
3   Putnam, 'The transnational and the text-searchable', 389.
4   The term 'Hansard' is also used for the transcripts of parliamentary debates in many Commonwealth countries.
5   Vice and Farrell, *The History of Hansard*, p. 18.
6   Vice and Farrell, *The History of Hansard*, p. 20.
7   Swartz, 'U.K. puts parliament proceedings online'.
8   Hansard 1803–2005, https://api.parliament.uk/historic-hansard/index.html (accessed 5 July 2020).
9   Hansard 1803–2005, https://api.parliament.uk/historic-hansard/index.html; University of Glasgow, *Historical Thesaurus of English*, https://ht.ac.uk/ (both accessed 5 July 2020).
10 Linking Parliamentary Records through Metadata, www.liparm.ac.uk (accessed 5 July 2020).
11 Digging into Linked Parliamentary Data, http://politicalmashup.nl/ (accessed 5 July 2020).
12 Hansard Online, https://hansard.parliament.uk/ (accessed 5 July 2020).
13 'About', Hansard Online, https://hansard.parliament.uk/about?historic=false (accessed 5 July 2020).
14 The Anglo-American Legal Tradition, http://aalt.law.uh.edu/ (accessed 5 July 2020).
15 Tanner *et al.*, 'Measuring mass text digitization, quality and usefulness'.
16 Holley, 'How good can it get?'.
17 'About this project', Old Bailey Proceedings Online, www.oldbaileyonline.org/static/Project.jsp (accessed 5 July 2020).
18 Staffordshire Historical Collection, British History Online, www.british-history.ac.uk/search/series/staffs-hist-collection (accessed 5 July 2020).
19 British Library Newspapers, www.gale.com/intl/c/british-library-newspapers-part-i (accessed 5 July 2020).
20 British Library, 'Heritage Made Digital' www.bl.uk/projects/heritage-made-digital (accessed 5 July 2020).
21 British Library, 'Heritage Made Digital – the newspapers'.
22 British Library, 'Heritage Made Digital – the newspapers'.
23 Tropy, https://tropy.org/ (accessed 5 July 2020).
24 Henry III Fine Rolls Project, https://finerollshenry3.org.uk/home.html (accessed 5 July 2020).
25 The *OED* dates 'crowdsourcing' to 2006, and defines it as 'The practice of obtaining information or services by soliciting input from a large number of people, typically via the internet and often without offering compensation' (www.oed.com/view/Entry/376403#eid288590739,

accessed 9 August 2019). The last aspect of this definition has since led to debate about the exploitative nature of some crowdsourcing activities, and there is now much more thoughtful consideration of co-creation and the shared generation of knowledge.

26 Hedges and Dunn, 'Crowd-Sourcing Scoping Study', pp. 2, 21.
27 'Newspapers and gazettes', Trove, https://trove.nla.gov.au/newspaper/ (accessed 5 July 2020).
28 'About', Trove, https://trove.nla.gov.au/about (accessed 5 July 2020).
29 'What's on the menu?', New York Public Library, http://menus.nypl.org/ (accessed 5 July 2020).
30 Operation War Diary, https://www.operationwardiary.org/ (accessed 5 July 2020).
31 READ: Recognition and Enhancement of Archival Documents, https://read.transkribus.eu/ (accessed 5 July 2020).
32 Transkribus, https://transkribus.eu/Transkribus/ (accessed 5 July 2020).
33 'Project update – so long to Transcribe Bentham', *Transcribe Bentham Blog* (6 December 2017), https://blogs.ucl.ac.uk/transcribe-bentham/category/read-project/ (accessed 5 July 2020).
34 'Project update – improving the automated recognition of Bentham's handwriting', https://blogs.ucl.ac.uk/transcribe-bentham/2018/11/28/project-update-automated-recognition-bentham-handwriting/ (accessed 5 July 2020).
35 Old Bailey search, www.oldbaileyonline.org/forms/formMain.jsp (accessed 5 July 2020).
36 Old Bailey API, www.oldbaileyonline.org/static/API.jsp (accessed 5 July 2020).
37 It should be noted, though, that Ancestry is open to working with academic researchers at the project level. Data from Ancestry and Findmypast, for example, has been included in the Digital Panopticon project, available at www.digitalpanopticon.org/ (accessed 5 July 2020).
38 'Using British History Online', British History Online, www.british-history.ac.uk/using-bho (accessed 5 July 2020).
39 'Introducing JSON', www.json.org/ (accessed 5 July 2020).
40 Historical Hansard API, https://api.parliament.uk/historic-hansard/api (accessed 5 July 2020).
41 Early English Books Online (EEBO), Text Creation Partnership, https://textcreationpartnership.org/tcp-texts/eebo-tcp-early-english-books-online/ (accessed 5 July 2020).
42 Oxford University Research Archive, 'EEBO-TCP Phase I texts (XML files TEI P3)', https://ora.ox.ac.uk/objects/uuid:ad7da8fc-cd8e-4637-

FORMULATING YOUR RESEARCH QUESTIONS 47

8b7c-99498436dbaa; GitHub Gist, 'Download all Github-archived EEBO-TCP xml files from their associated repositories on Github', https://gist.github.com/mjlavin80/506d58f0b8183e8804b29446424e5118 (both accessed 5 July 2020).
43 For an introduction to the principles, see Blaney, 'Introduction to the principles of linked open data'.
44 The British Library has, for example, secured the personal archives of a number of individuals – among them the poet Wendy Cope, the publisher Carmen Callil and the writers Hanif Kureishi and Will Self – which contain papers, but also emails, floppy disks and computer hard drives.
45 'Frequently asked questions', UK Web Archive, www.webarchive.org.uk/en/ukwa/info/faq (accessed 5 July 2020).
46 'About us', UK Web Archive, www.webarchive.org.uk/en/ukwa/info/about (accessed 30 October 2020).
47 O'Neil, *Weapons of Math Destruction*, p. 21. Elsewhere O'Neil notes that appeals to the objectivity of an algorithm can be a useful misdirection from a decision actually taken by a person (p. 133). On the racial biases of search engines, see Noble, *Algorithms of Oppression*.
48 'Example: Kress email release', Electronic Records, George W. Bush Presidential Library, www.georgewbushlibrary.smu.edu/en/Research/Presidential-Records/White-House-Email (accessed 5 July 2020).
49 There is a rapidly developing historiography if you are interested in exploring this further, including, for example: Brügger and Milligan, *The SAGE Handbook of Web History*, and Brügger and Schroeder, *The Web as History*.
50 Gentzkow *et al.*, 'Text as data', 2.
51 'meta-, *prefix*', *OED*, www.oed.com/view/Entry/117150 (accessed 29 October 2020).
52 Gartner, *Metadata*, introduces the topic with plenty of historical context.
53 Early English Books Online, https://about.proquest.com/products-services/databases/eebo.html (accessed 30 October 2020).
54 Milligan, 'Lost in the infinite archive'.

✥ 3 ✦

HOW A DIGITAL PROJECT BEGINS

In digital humanities, the notion of scholarly work tends to be wider than in normalized forms of academic output, such as monographs and academic papers.[1]

How do you get the text you want to work with, whether it is in a book on a shelf or comes from a Twitter account, into usable form? This chapter outlines the process and the choices involved. Although we will touch on topics to do with text manipulation, structure and version control, this is a high-level overview and we will look at working with text itself in detail in chapters 4 and 5. In Chapter 6 we will discuss caring for your data over the whole life of the project and in Chapter 7 deriving visual outputs, such as charts and maps, from all of that work.

INTRODUCTION TO THE POST OFFICE DIRECTORIES

Throughout this book we will be focusing on one historical document so that we can show how different approaches to it can be taken. We have chosen *The Post Office London Directory for 1879*. All the files we will use throughout the book are available in our companion repository, if you wish to replicate what we have done. Appendix 1 describes how to get a copy of the data. The approach taken here will, we hope, map onto using many other types of historical data.

The Post Office directory for London was first published in 1800, although other directories had been published since the seventeenth century for London and other cities throughout Great Britain and Ireland. By 1850 the Post Office directories had a standard structure, which included things like a trade directory (an alphabetical listing of tradespeople) and a 'court' directory (a listing of people who were not in trade, whose addresses were purely residential). For this book we are going to use the street-by-street listing which details streets alphabetically, with a 'postman's walk' described for it. Crucially at each domestic address an occupant is listed. The compass point and listing of adjoining streets additionally allows us to orient ourselves on the historical street. It is therefore possible to place residents and businesses quite precisely on a part of a street in a given year.

Our directory comes from the time just before that identified by Peter Atkins as peak coverage for the London Post Office directory,[2] but we should not imagine that it is comprehensive. As Figure 3.1 shows, only one occupant is listed for each address, so from the directory alone we can have no idea of the identity or even the number of other people living in the properties. As well as errors and gaps in the information

Blenheim road, *St. John's wood* (**N.W.**), *between* 42 & 44 *Abbey rd.* MAP F 6, G 6.

1 Thornton James
2 Goodiff Francis Taylor
4 Padwick Miss
5 Chapman William
6 Archer John Chapman
7 Martin Samuel H
8 Webster Mrs
9 Cheshire John, professor of music
10 Watson Hugh
11 Hurle Capt. Arthur
12 Smith Mrs
14 Wright Miss
15 Abrams Benjamin
.... *here is Loudoun road* ....
16 Vokes Frederick
17 Crick Mrs
18 Alpe Edmund Nicholas
19 Kennedy Mrs. W. H
20 Urquhart Mrs. & Miss
21 Brunskill John
22 Seymour George Lim, artist
23 Millett HannibalCurnow, solicitr
24 MacLeod Norman
25 Hughes Harley
26 de Fivas Alan S
27 Jacox Miss
28 White Charles John
29 Peake Mrs

Figure 3.1 Blenheim Road in *The Post Office London Directory for 1879*

collection process – which was done by agents knocking at doors and writing down details – the directories also show biases such as providing more details for more affluent areas and professions.[3]

This is a good reminder that datasets are always shaped by the contingent circumstances of their creation and curation. In this case the information was collected by a commercial publisher to be sold to a particular market. As we would expect, that commercial motive leaves its mark on the data we have to work with.

We should also repeat again here our claim made in Chapter 1 that digital approaches in no way supersede other forms of historical research. A historian interested in a particular neighbourhood in Victorian London would, of course, bring to bear many separate lines of evidence and try to compensate for the collection biases that Atkins describes.

Nevertheless, given the richness of this data, the possibilities are enormous. For concision we will only use part of the 1878 London directory, but the potential for comparative studies across time and across cities and towns in the UK is clear. For example, a researcher interested in the changing socioeconomic profile of a street over the decades of the nineteenth century could extract the business and residential information from successive annual editions of the Post Office directory. Of course, we do not necessarily need digital tools to do this for one street: it is quite possible to sit with a directory for each of a span of decades and list the businesses given for that street and its ratio of residential to commercial use. At scale though, this becomes prohibitively laborious. If, for example, we wanted to compare the number of lawyers in London and Edinburgh throughout the nineteenth century, the task is daunting. Even more difficult, with pen and paper, would be to count the genders of named individuals (women are given gendered titles, such as 'Mrs' in the directory, whereas men generally have no titles).

All this becomes feasible once we have the text in a machine-readable form, but there is still work to be done.

SCANNING THE DIRECTORY

The first stage in any digital history project that focuses on textual material is to acquire or create a machine-readable version of the data. By machine-readable we mean that text-based software can understand it *as text*. For example, a photograph of a page of text might be a digital object readable by image software such as Photoshop, but Photoshop cannot search for words within that photograph. Some smartphone apps can now read the text of photographs by processing it behind the scenes to make it machine-readable. This obscures the distinction, but the distinction is still there and the work needs to be done somewhere in the process.

Ideally, we want the text to be readable in a form by *any* editor, but proprietary formats (such as Microsoft Word) are often used by default. In Chapter 4 we will explain why formats such as Word are not suitable for many of the tasks we will cover in this book and suggest a free alternative.

Historians are often happy to discover that a particular text is available in machine-readable form, even if they do not think of it in those terms, because this means that someone else has done the work of producing it. Whenever a print text is made available online, whether for searching or for download, someone has produced a machine-readable version of that text.

For a digital project, finding that required texts are available in machine-readable form is usually a great advantage. The downside is that the original decisions made about how exactly it was produced may not suit the new project; and sometimes, unfortunately, the work required to manipulate the data into the desired form may be more costly than having the source digitised anew.

We do not have any existing machine-readable files at all for this project. All we have is a print copy of the 1878 directory. Our first task, then, is to scan the book so that we have digital images of the pages. For this book we had 100 pages scanned by a scanning company, at a cost of £13. Companies such as the one we used can advise on format and quality, but we had our pages scanned as *bitonal*, which means that each part of the page is either black or white with no gradations (as in *greyscale*). Although less legible and pleasant to read than greyscale, bitonal scans are smaller, which becomes an important consideration if you are scanning in bulk. The file format we asked for was TIF, which is the recommended archival format for images. The resolution was 400 DPI (dots per inch, which equates to the detail scanned and, therefore, the extent to which it is possible to zoom without losing sharpness). The minimal resolution for archival-quality images is 300 DPI, but nowadays a higher resolution is often used. Figure 3.1 is from one of our scans.

You can scan pages yourself and produce good results with care, but this can be time-consuming and error-prone. Delicate materials and non-standard formats or sizes may require specialist equipment. Many libraries and archives allow photographing of their holdings as long as the object is properly treated. That might mean being rested on foam wedges to form a cradle for photographing opened pages and with pages held open by specially designed weights.

A quality check of the scans is an important, though dull, job to do before going any further. You can verify that the right number of pages have been scanned quite easily, and you can check for duplicates automatically (see Appendix 2 for how to do this). But you will need to look through each page to make sure there are no legibility problems. Common scanning mistakes include cutting off part of the text or text being obscured by objects such as fingers, and blurring as the text curves down into the book's gutter.

OCR AND REKEYING

For some purposes, images alone are sufficient. But for this project we need to be able to work with the text itself. There are essentially two ways to produce text from images, as we described in the previous chapter. It is an important distinction so we will reiterate it. A person or people can simply type out what they see, word by word, page by page; this is rekeying. Or a computer program can attempt to convert the pixels in the image to text; this is OCR.

Rekeying is resource-intensive. You can pay someone to transcribe the text, transcribe it yourself or try to persuade others to do it (students, for credit; members of the public, for personal interest). In almost all cases the transcribers need to be competent at reading the text and accurately typing it. The exceptions are those rare 'crowdsourcing' projects which are open to the public and successful enough to get multiple transcriptions of the same text, compensating for individual misreadings by the sheer number of readings provided. Crowdsourcing has costs of its own: there has to be a mechanism for transcriptions to be uploaded, possibly checked, collated with other versions and for progress to be tracked; credit needs to be carefully considered and therefore requires closer monitoring of individual contributions.

OCR is much cheaper. There are numerous free programs which can do it. Why, then, does anyone bother with rekeying? Because OCR is still, in many cases, quite inaccurate. A cleanly printed text with a modern typeface and a rectilinear text block will OCR well, but most historical printed texts are not like that. Handwriting is still an enormous challenge to OCR programs, although, as described in Chapter 2, impressive results are now being obtained.

There are a number of ways to increase the accuracy of OCR. First is pre-processing the images to make them more suitable for OCR, which includes things like sharpening the text, increasing the contrast and, possibly, changing the images from greyscale to bitonal. These things can be done in an image editor. A more advanced technique is to OCR the same text with three different OCR programs and then compare the outputs, the majority decision being assumed more likely to be correct. A similar process is often used in rekeying: two transcripts are compared and any divergence checked against the original text.

For the purposes of this book we have OCRed the 'B' section of the street directory ourselves for comparative purposes. We have also had the same part of the book rekeyed by a specialist keying company, which cost £260. Recall that scanning the same material cost £13 and you will understand why many digital resources present images only, or images and OCR. Rekeying is more expensive than OCR but, despite improvements in the latter, should produce much better results. The files for both methods are available in our repository, and we would encourage you to compare the two.

In the repository you will find two folders with different versions of the rekeyed text: one in a structured form and one in unstructured form. We will show you ways of working with unstructured text in Chapter 4, and Chapter 5 will cover structured text. For now, be aware that if you ask keying companies to produce a text with a structure, you will have to specify exactly what that structure is.

Our keying instructions are in the repository for reference, but if you contact a keying company, they will tell you what kind of instructions they need or provide a template for you to customise. At this point you also need to agree the accuracy of the keying. Unless the text is particularly difficult to read, 99.9% is normally a minimum: this is the kind of accuracy that can be attained with human transcription but rarely with OCR.

GIT AND VERIFICATION

The first thing we will do on receipt of the keyed files is to put them under version control. How to do this is explained in detail in Chapter 6. Version control gives us two advantages. First, if we find a problem while working on the files, we can determine if this is something we introduced or if it came from errors by the keyers. Under version control we can revert the state of the files to the point at which we originally received them, or to any other commits. Second, when working with files, especially in bulk, mistakes are common. Making mistakes is a good way to learn, especially if you know you can restore your files to an earlier version, giving you the freedom to experiment. This is what version control brings. We will use and recommend a free version-control program called Git. Git requires you to write a message describing the status of your files every time you create a point to which you might want to revert. Used systematically, this is an extremely useful way of documenting and tracking your progress.

With structural data supplied by keying companies, you should first check that you actually have the structure you asked for. At this point you should probably check the accuracy of the keying: you may need to send it back, so this is best done before starting any other work. Projects normally sample the text and proof it against the original, either choosing to proof a percentage of the pages or file size, or a couple of sample sections. In our experience, keying companies provide an excellent service but their work will need to be checked.

If you have chosen to use OCR for your transcription then a similar process applies. You will need to check a sample the text produced by the OCR and proof it against the original to establish its accuracy. Instead of sending it back to keyers, though, you will need to fix it yourself or, if this is not feasible, decide to use it and work around its limitations. Initially rekeying is more resource-intensive than OCR, but you might find that if you count the hours subsequently spent on the OCR process, the resource differences are not so clear cut.

TYPOGRAPHIC CLEANING

Cleaning text is a fact of life when using OCR. You may have to do a bit of this with rekeying if there are legitimate reasons why the keyers did not key the text accurately and fully. Sometimes, damaged pages in the original text results in gaps; legibility can be lost through scanning errors; keyers cannot capture any text which has been omitted by mistake. This is why we emphasised the importance of checking scans prior to OCR or keying: illegibility or missing text caused by scanning problems will be your problem, not that of the keyers.

It may also turn out that your instructions to the keyers were not as comprehensive or unambiguous as you thought, and there are now some changes that you want or some enhancements you will need to make to the text. With a large amount of text, however carefully you examine it, there are always likely to be special features or subtle inconsistencies which only become evident when someone has to type it all out. Do not feel you have failed if you have to do some work to address such problems after keying or OCR: they are a common trade-off in the digitisation process.

When you look through OCRed text you will begin to notice patterns to at least some of the errors. Finding and changing patterns in text usually means it is time for *regular expressions*. Regular expressions, or regex, will be quite a large part of this book because they are a tool that will frequently save you time and effort. Many software programs for working with text incorporate regex, so they are something of a general-purpose tool. Regex can appear arcane at first but getting to grips with them is one of the biggest productivity boosts you can give yourself when working with text.

A common OCR error with some typefaces is that the letter o is confused with the numeral 0. You might see things like this:

```
R0bert
```

or

```
19o5
```

It is a fair bet that a 0 surrounded by letters is an OCR error, as is an o surrounded by numbers. Regex, introduced in Chapter 4, will find these patterns and many, many others.

You can fix many OCR or other transcription problems in this way. You might not, though, want to go ahead and use regex just to change all those zeroes to the letter o, because some examples could be correct as they are. What you should do instead is use regex to create a list of all the examples of the pattern, along with the context. Delete the false positives and you will be left with a file of changes that you know are safe.

Using regex will certainly speed up the process of correcting OCR, but we cannot pretend that it is a painless process and some types of errors are not amenable to being fixed this way. In Chapter 7 we will discuss some cleaning we did of lists of occupations we extracted from the rekeyed Post Office directory data. As you can see, this was mostly manual work, iterating through lists of occupations and fixing inconsistencies by eye.

Sometimes you will find yourself semi-automating corrections: using tools like regex to do some of the work and focusing your manual interventions on more difficult cases. There will also be diminishing returns as your text is improved, and at some point you will have to stop this work and move on. In our experience, cleaning data is almost always a large part of digital history projects.[4]

ADDING STRUCTURE WITH REGEX

In our Post Office directory the majority of addresses begin with a number at the beginning of a line, so we could use this known pattern to mark a number at the beginning of a line as the beginning of an address (we will explore how this is done in the next two chapters). For this task we would again use regex, which is perfect for things like finding any number at the beginning of a line. The amount of structure that it is possible to add in this way depends on the number of readily identifiable patterns that the text exhibits.

If you are working with OCRed text which is regular in structure, you can build up regex to add tagging to textual features. The more irregularities the text exhibits, which may be because of typographical errors or simply real-world variety in the data, the more manual checking and cleaning you will need to do, and the harder it is to define patterns which work effectively.

You are unlikely ever to be able to automate cleaning and adding structure with perfect results. Textual data tends to be messy and inconsistent, and some outliers will evade the most carefully crafted automated process. It is quite normal to combine automation with manual interventions. A sequence you might well go through looks like this:

1. Investigate the data and find a pattern
2. Automate your changes

3. Search to check for errors or outliers
4. Manually fix the items found in 3, if small in number
5. Go back to 1

At first, working with text in an automated way might seem intimidating. In the following chapters we aim to show you, step by step, how to go about it. With practice and experience it can become second nature.

NOTES

1 Berry and Fagerjord, *Digital Humanities*, p. 28.
2 Atkins, *The Directories of London: 1677–1977*.
3 Atkins, *The Directories of London: 1677–1977*, pp. 126–131.
4 Hill and Hengchen, 'Quantifying the impact of dirty OCR on historical text analysis', fn2, briefly discusses the common claim that data cleaning takes up 80% of a digital project, although they can find no evidence for this particular ratio. Naturally, the amount of cleaning required will vary from project to project. See also D'Ignazio and Klein, *Data Feminism*, pp. 130–135, on the 'mythos' of data cleaning.

4

WORKING WITH TEXT 1: UNSTRUCTURED TEXT

> This discipline has to do with Grammar, because whatever is worthy of remembrance is committed to writing.[1]

Many definitions of history, from Isidore of Seville onwards, assume that history is centred around text. Even those historians who focus wholly on non-written sources (some archaeologists, for example) use written secondary materials, including finding aids and peer literature, and produce text themselves in the form of emails, notes, drafts, reports and peer-reviewed texts. The techniques we describe in this chapter can be applied not just to textual material that you acquire but also reflexively to textual material that you produce yourself.

These techniques may be quite different from anything you have used before, but if you spend some time practising them you will have a toolkit that allows you to perform powerful operations on collections of text, large or small.

In this chapter we will sometimes use 'data' as a shorthand for 'textual data', by which we mean text in any machine-readable form (normally in files of various formats). However, the techniques we describe here are not computational, in the sense that you could not use them to, for example, find the mean value from a set of figures.

KNOWING THE CONTEXT OF THE DATA

As a historian, you know that understanding the context in which information was gathered and recorded is essential to working with it. To work with a particular set of taxation records, for example, it would be important to know who was liable for the tax and who was not and the process for claiming or achieving exemption, how the assessments were made and over what period, and what opportunities there might have been to game the system to avoid or evade tax. If you work in detail with such records, you will probably come to learn how many scribes there were and their different habits; perhaps, for example, Scribe C made more thorough notes than Scribe A. Finally, you will have a good idea of what is not known about the records and how they were produced, and will keep that in mind in any evaluation of the evidence they provide.

As Tim Hitchcock cautions, although trained historians also understand the context and limitations of libraries, archives and printed editions that may house these primary texts, they are not necessarily so skilled with digital resources:

> We can now engage with that new resource in new ways, but to do so we need scholars who can work with old sources in their new digital guise, and who recognise that digital makes them different.[2]

The digital format of records is, then, something to be understood in the same way. That understanding should become part of the historian's toolkit. There are, however, two problems with this 'should' claim: historians are still not routinely trained to understand and work with digital records, and digital records are often poorly documented, making their production and methodology hard to reconstruct and understand.

A common and useful distinction is made between data which is 'born digital' and digitised data, which has been converted somehow from analogue form (usually print or manuscript). A frequent assumption is that born-digital data is easier to work with but this is rarely the case. Let us take a very simple example of a piece of born-digital data to show the complexity of dealing with it:

```
{"created_at": "Mon Aug 20 14:27:45 +0000 2018", "id":
1031548347633618946, "id_str": "1031548347633618946",
"fulltext": "RT @j_w_baker: Thread. Or, why build-
ing our emerging digital scholarly practice around
well-meaning but opaque commercial platforms is foll\
u2026"…
```

This is a tweet from the timeline of the account @bho_history, retweeting @j_w_baker. We have only given the first 270 characters for reasons of space, because the full tweet is 9,150 characters, in the format in which Twitter allows us to export, which is JSON, mentioned in Chapter 2.

Working with hundreds of thousands or millions of such tweets is challenging, and Twitter is inherently a very simple, constrained and predictable format!

Part of the problem is that born-digital data was almost never created with the needs of humanities scholars in mind. It may be very verbose and need stripping down before it can be used. It may require some technical work to make it usable at all (for example, it may be stored in the form of individual database tables that need to be joined together correctly). It may well be poorly documented, meaning that some aspects of the data, like the field codes used, are quite opaque.

Some digitised textual historical records may be more easily used because they were actually intended for historians. Here the problems are more likely to be about the selection of the data (what was digitised and what was omitted?) and the methodology (OCR or rekeyed? – a distinction we have already addressed). What quality assurance, if any, was done? If printed copies were digitised, where did they come from? Were problems with the edition used corrected with reference to other copies? Have any errors been silently corrected? As you can see, good documentation would answer many of these questions, but, as we must admit from our own experience, producing good documentation is often regarded as a luxury by hard-pressed digitisation projects.

Beyond the context of the data, you will probably want to know something about the accuracy of transcription and if any subsequent data manipulation was done (or if you need to make changes yourself). If software was used, what was it and how was it configured and its results verified? If people in the text have been identified, was this done by manual intervention or by a piece of software? And what rules were used to determine what constitutes a person? Is John Bull a person? Is a ghost a person? Is the Holy Ghost a person?

You will not always be able to answer these questions, but you should always be ready to ask them.

PLAIN TEXT

In this book we talk a lot about 'text' and 'text files', but by that we do not mean the kind of text you read in a Word document or on a PowerPoint slide. There is an important distinction here between text that can be read by many kinds of software, which we will call 'plain text', which can be ready by any *text editor*, and text that can only be read by specific

WORKING WITH TEXT 1: UNSTRUCTURED TEXT

Table 4.1 Common file formats

File extension	Format	Plain text?
.doc, docx	word processing	no
.xsl, .xslx	spreadsheets	no
.txt	any text	yes
.xml	XML	yes
.csv, .tsv	comma-separated or tab-separated values	yes

software, such as Microsoft Word or Pages on a Mac. Compared to these latter programs, text editors look a bit different, seeming comparatively unadorned because they omit typographic features such as font changes.

Why are we insisting on this distinction? First, because plain text is susceptible to manipulation in ways that a Word file is not. It is in Microsoft's interest for everyone to buy their Office software and so they make it difficult for people without the right software to use the file. Plain text is in no one's proprietary format and can be read by many – often free – tools. Second, because one of the techniques we want to evangelise in this chapter is that of passing text from one tool to another, so that each specialist tool works with plain text and produces plain text for the next tool. Third, because programs like Word will not deal well with some of the formats we will address, or will actually corrupt them.

Table 4.1 covers only a very few formats, but if you want to know if a file is plain text, there is an easy way to find out: open the file in a text editor. If you see readable and sensible-looking text, it is plain text; if you see apparent nonsense, it is probably not.

What, though, is a text editor? Every PC has at least one: a Windows machine probably has WordPad and Notepad and a Mac may have TextEdit. However, at this point we are going to strongly urge you to download another text editor. This is because to follow along with this book you will need a text editor that allows you to do some fancy find-and-replace work using *regular expressions*, which will be explained soon. Fortunately, there are many excellent and free text editors, so it is easy to try a few and find one you like. Text editors are the workhorses of digital tools and can excite strong opinions, but it really does not matter which one you choose as long as it has regular expression support, and nearly all do. If you do not know where to start, we would suggest trying Sublime Text (www.sublimetext.com), which is free for evaluation purposes.

While we are tooling up, there are two more free pieces of software you will need to follow along with what we cover in this chapter: a *command line interface* (CLI), and the version-control tool Git. See the appropriate text box for your operating system for how to get the CLI and Git.

> **Mac or Linux**. Good news: you already have the command line. On a Mac it is called 'Terminal'; it is somewhat hidden, but type 'terminal' into Finder and you will get it. On most versions of Linux, you can bring up the command line with the keyboard shortcut ctrl+alt+t.
>
> Git has a package for Mac: https://git-scm.com/download/mac. On Linux, you can install Git from your package manager.

> **Windows** comes with its own default CLI, usually known as DOS; but it is so different, and so comparatively limited, that we cannot use it in this book. A better Windows command line, called PowerShell, is worth exploring if you are a committed Windows user, but it is also too different for use in this book.
>
> We recommend instead that you download a free command line tool called Git Bash, which comes as part of Git for Windows (https://gitforwindows.org/). Once it is installed, you will be able to right-click on any folder in Windows Explorer and see an option to open Git Bash in that folder.
>
> You can install both the CLI and Git in one go by downloading Git for Windows from https://git-scm.com/download/win and installing the single executable.

> **Raspberry Pi**. A final option for trying out the command line is to get a small computer like a Raspberry Pi. You can get the cheapest models for less than £10, but we suggest making sure you get one with Wi-Fi. You will also need the right peripherals: connecting leads and an external keyboard, monitor (a television can be used for this) and probably a mouse; you can reuse existing peripherals, of course.
>
> Install the default operating system, Raspberry Pi OS, and it will come with the command line ready and available for text-processing work.

To follow along with our examples, which we would strongly recommend, you will need to take a copy of the data from this book's repository on GitHub:

```
https://github.com/ihr-digital/digital-history
```

The data you will find here is primarily the rekeyed pages of the 'B' streets from the Post Office directory, a process described in the previous chapter. Within the folder data you can find plain text transcriptions, which we will be using throughout this chapter. The folder XML is the same material but 'marked up', and these marked-up files will be the focus of the next chapter.

You will find a button on the main page for the repository called 'Clone or download', which you can use to download a zip file of all the data we will be working with. More detailed information on getting this data, including how to use the clone option, is given in Appendix 1.

WORKING WITH THE TEXT

In this section we will begin to introduce tools for working with text at scale. The techniques will work with any collection of plain text that you can fit on your computer, such as the Hansard material mentioned in Chapter 2. But as you become more familiar and comfortable with these approaches, you will, we hope, find yourself using them for small tasks on individual files too. An indispensable part of working with plain text is regular expressions, so we will start with them.

Regular expressions are a powerful way of searching and manipulating text. Crucially, they can find patterns in text such as:

- every number inside round brackets
- every capitalised word
- 'Mr' followed by one or more capitalised words (i.e. a crude name search)

From now on we will refer to them as '*regex*' – a common abbreviation that is useful to know if you are doing a web search on this topic.

The tricky aspect of learning regex is that these patterns are expressed in a terse way. This is off-putting at first, but do not be discouraged.

Please do not think, 'I don't have the right kind of brain for this'. You do. But your brain needs practice.

The best way to learn regex is to try out commands yourself on text that you are particularly interested in. For the following examples, we will use one file from our repository, `Balls-pond-road.txt`, which is in the folder `text-files`. We encourage you not only to follow along with this file, but to try to modify the examples with texts and questions of your own choosing as well.

Open the file `Balls-pond-road.txt` with your text editor of choice. Now you will need to locate two things: the find-and-replace tool in your editor and the option there to switch regex on or off. If you are using Sublime Text, the search box appears at the bottom of the screen and the regex button is to the extreme left of it, as in Figure 4.1, marked '.*'.

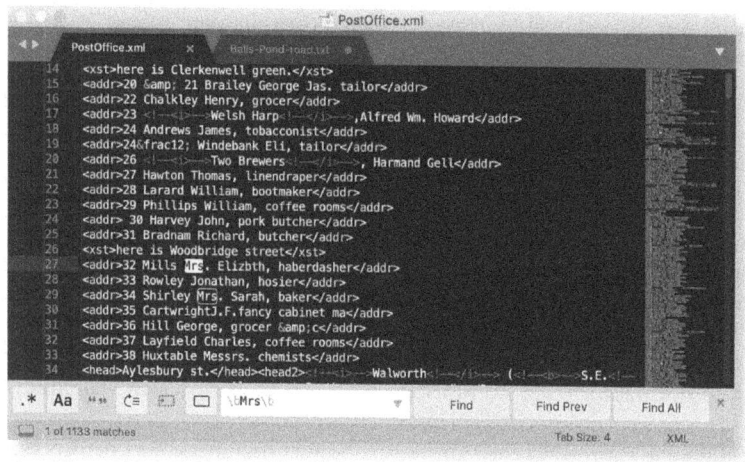

Figure 4.1 Sublime Text

Keep regex turned off for the moment. Now search the file for the number digit 1. Sublime Text highlights all matches, the first being the beginning of the address of John Clarke, Baker. You are already very familiar with this type of search, and probably familiar with its limitations as well. This is a literal string search ('string' means a sequence of any characters of any length) and you have to know in advance exactly what you want to find. Notice that the next highlight is from the address of Stokes, Nathaniel, Hosier, which is actually two separate highlights for the two digits in the number 11.

Case study:
patterns of addresses in the directory

One of the things we know about the Post Office directories is that information was not collected for every property and that more affluent areas and professions are better represented than poorer ones.[3] Given this, some historical questions we can ask might be:

- Can we derive information about the type of properties in a street and how they have been recorded?
- Can we estimate the completeness of collection for streets?
- Can we discover anything from the ratio of building names to numbers, or from the occurrence of addresses of the type 123A, 123B?

For all of these questions, regex is a tool we can use.

To begin our investigation of address patterns, we need to go beyond finding digits like 1, or fixed strings of digits like 123, to finding strings only consisting of any of the digits.

Now you need to turn on the regex option in your editor's search box. Instead of 1, we can now find any single digit: in regex anything within square brackets is an option for the match. Try searching for

```
[1234567890]
```

This means 'find 1 or 2 or 3 or ...'. If you have regex turned off, this will fail because there is no entry with this literal string of characters: no house number is [1234567890]. But if you keep hitting find with regex turned on, you should see your editor finding each digit in the file in turn because it is now matching a pattern. This, in essence, is all regex is.

Any character can go in square brackets. Try that out yourself to get a firm idea of how it works. In regex, everything inside square brackets is a possible match. If it helps, you can mentally insert the word 'or' between each character inside square brackets.

In the example above, we made you type out all the numbers. If you want to search for any letter you could equally type all twenty-six inside square brackets, thus searching for 'a' or 'b' or ... you get the idea. But there are abbreviations for regex searches for ranges of letters and numbers because they are so common:

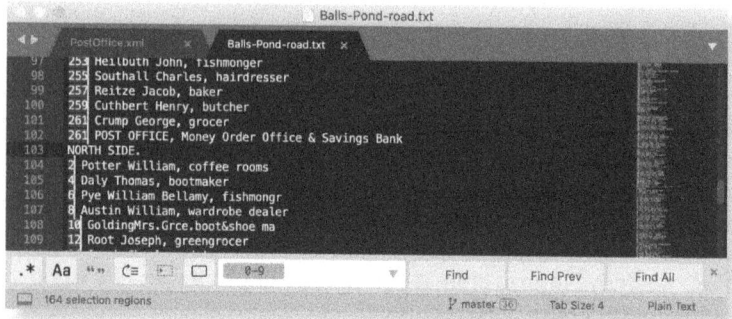

Figure 4.2 The Ball's Pond Road .txt file in Sublime Text with all numbers highlighted by regex search for [0-9]

```
[a-z]
[A-Z]
[0-9]
```

Try that last search: you should get the same result for [0-9] as for [1234567890].

This search is still matching individual digits. Our historical task is to find all the address numbers, however long or short they are. To express 'however short or long', regex uses a plus symbol '+'. This is one of the three regex quantifiers, and it means 'one or more of the preceding'. The preceding might be a single character or it might be a group of characters, like all digits. Try this search:

```
[0-9]+
```

This matches any string of numbers and stops when it comes to anything which is not a number. We give you all three regex quantifiers in table 4.2 for reference. But the one to remember, because you will use it all the time, is +.

Table 4.2 Quantifiers in regular expressions

Quantifier	Meaning
+	one or more
?	one or none
*	none or any

You have probably noticed that we are matching too much here; because we searched for any number, we get the map references at the top of the file. This is a common problem when working with unstructured text: it can be hard to define exactly what you want. Fortunately, in this case there is something which defines all the address numbers we are interested in: they all occur at the beginning of a line. In regex you can specify the beginning of a line with ^. This caret symbol anchors the string so it only matches when at the beginning of a line. Try this:

`^[0-9]+`

We said earlier that regex is terse, and now you can see why!

Happily, this expression contains all the main ideas used in regex searches: an anchor (^, where the match can occur), a character class ([], a list of what is allowed to match) and a quantifier (+, how much to match).

Now that we have a sense of what regex does, let us try to put more detail on our historical questions above. Confining ourselves just to the patterns of numbers in files, here are a few approaches that have occurred to us. You can probably come up with others.

- Are there equal numbers of odd and even house numbers for a street? If so, does that suggest the street is well sampled and, therefore, more likely to be more affluent?
- What is the ratio of addresses like 123A to addresses which contain simply numbers? Does that tell us anything about the type of street it is? Do more subdivided buildings tell us something about the social class of the inhabitants? But does the collection methodology discussed by Peter Atkins in his book about the directories (only one entry was collected per address; more collection was done in prosperous areas)[4] mean that this information is lost from the data?
- Can we compare the number of addresses in a file to the number of expected addresses? If we can do this, does it serve as a proxy for how well sampled the street was? For example, a street with only twenty lines but whose highest number is 30 is likely to be better sampled than one with fifty lines but whose highest number is 95. (This is complicated by the fact that the last address number in each file is not necessarily the highest.)

To answer these questions, we will now start to use regex outside of the text editor, on the command line. This will allow us to do more powerful things with the results of our searches and also to work on multiple files at once.

We introduced regex in a text editor first, to give you a tangible sense of how it works. But where regex in a text editor really shines is in find and replace. Just as you can find patterns, you can also replace with a pattern as well. For example, you might want every paragraph in a piece of continuous prose to end with a full point. Rather than proofreading or scanning, you could use regex to find every word followed directly by the end of a paragraph and replace them with the same word followed by a full point. It does not matter what the words are: each individual find-and-replace action finds a word and replaces it with that word and a full point.

Using regex can make manipulating an individual file an automatic process rather than a manual chore, as long as you can reliably identify a find pattern and a replace pattern. It would be remiss of us if we did not let you in on this time-saver, so you will find an example below. Try it out in your text editor before you move on to the next section.

FIND AND REPLACE

For this example, we will mark all of the numbered addresses in the `Balls-pond-road.txt` file with the words 'House number: ' (note the space after the colon). To find the numbers we want, our search is:

```
^[0-9]+
```

As you know, this matches any number of digits at the beginning of a line. Each time we find a house number, whatever that particular number is, we want to put text in front of it. This means we actually need to replace the number *with itself* in each case. To do this, we put brackets around the entire search:

```
(^[0-9]+)
```

Try carrying out a find and replace with this in the find field and the replace field left empty: you will see that all the numbers are deleted. In

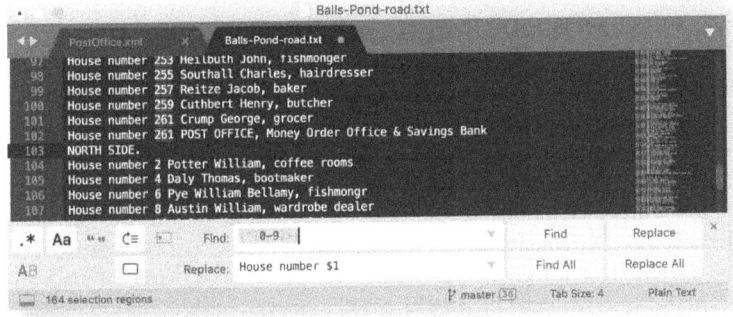

Figure 4.3 Addition of 'House number' in Sublime Text using regex find (`^[0-9]+`) replace `House number $1`

order to retain the numbers, in the replace box we can refer to what was found in the brackets with `$1` and precede it with our new text:

```
House number $1
```

`$1` is the convention for referring to the first set of brackets, known as a capture group. If you add a second set you can recall what is in those brackets with `$2`, and so on.[5]

What we have done here is a simple form of a markup. We have marked something of particular interest in the text in a consistent way to make it easier to investigate. We could even give the files to someone who does not know or want to use regex and they would be able to find the material with a literal text search for 'House number'.

As always, we would encourage you to practise replacement using expressions. First get comfortable with one set of brackets and then try with two or even three sets. For example, you can swap the order in your replacement with:

```
$2$1
```

This puts the content matched second in front of the content matched first. Anything not included in brackets at all is deleted.

INTRODUCTION TO THE COMMAND LINE

The command line is a text-only window that allows you to interact with a computer by typing commands.[6] That might not sound like much, but the command line is central to the techniques we want this book to teach. You can perform complex tasks on the command line by typing in a few words. The command line allows you to work with thousands of files at once, if you need to. For a historian wishing to work with a collection of texts, it is an ideal tool. Figure 4.4 gives an example of what the command line typically looks like.

If you choose to, you can use this text interface to do almost anything you can do with the more familiar graphical user interfaces (GUIs) like web browsers, email programs or media players, as well as system-wide things like listing folders or copying files. We will spend a lot of time on search in this chapter and the next, and there are times, particularly with large text collections, where a text editor would not cope but the command line easily could.[7]

When open, the command line will present you with a prompt, as in Figure 4.4, where the character $ indicates that you can type something.

Figure 4.4 The command line

Here you can type a command and press return. When you type a valid command, a program is run. This is the source of the command line's power: there are thousands of programs that can be run from it with a command consisting of one or two words. Many of these programs are often quite simple in themselves, written according to the principle 'do one thing well'. As we will see later, you can daisy-chain these simple programs together to great effect.

If you learn a programming language such as Python, you can write a program that will do the same thing as any command line program. But these in-built command line programs are written in a faster language than Python and are very efficient. If you do want to learn to code, replicating command line programs is useful for learning, but for everyday use this would be to reinvent a slower and more cumbersome wheel.

As well as being very fast and flexible, the command line treats you like an adult. This means it will not ask you, 'Are you sure you want to do this?' It will simply execute the command you give it. If you ask it to delete or overwrite an important file, it will instantly do so. If you use the command line frequently, at some point it is highly likely you will make a mistake. When working on files that are important to you (rather than experimenting), read back what you have typed before pressing return and be sure that you understand what it does. As always with important files, you should have a plan for how you are going to restore the situation if things go wrong. The reason we enthuse about Git (see Chapter 6) is that between us, the authors of this book, we have made lots of mistakes and Git has often been our saviour. Git allows you to restore a folder to the way it was at previous points in its history, including before you deleted an important file!

It is curious that many humanities researchers, who work with text in very sophisticated ways, find the command line intimidating or unintuitive. With a very few commands and an understanding of how to pass output from one command to another, an enormous amount can be accomplished by those willing to give it a try.

If you have installed, or found, your command line software as detailed above, open it up now. It will open at a default location, which may not be a convenient one. On Windows you can right-click in a folder, and the context menu will offer to open the command line right there (it will say something like 'Open Git Bash here' or 'Open Terminal here'). On a Mac you can open the Terminal and, having found the folder you want in Finder, drag Finder into the Terminal window and the Terminal will insert the path to the folder.

Figure 4.5 The default Mac Terminal

Figure 4.6 Git Bash

WORKING WITH TEXT 1: UNSTRUCTURED TEXT

The first thing you often want to do is to check your location. Essentially, the command line is always pointing at a folder. So, here's our first command: `pwd` (if it helps to remember it, it stands for 'print working directory'). Type `pwd` into the command line and press return. A common result for `pwd` when writing this chapter was:

```
/home/jb/repos/digital-history
```

We were keeping the text of this book in a Git repository called `digital-history`. Your location will be something different. But wherever you are, you might want to move somewhere else. If you look at the folder path above you will see that the next level up is called 'repos'. On the command line you move up one level, to the parent folder, with this command:

```
cd ..
```

The `cd` stands for 'change directory' ('directory' is the Unix term for what Windows calls a folder; in this book we are using 'folder'). If, instead of typing `cd ..`, you type `cd` followed by the name of a subfolder, you will move *down* one level into that directory. Remember that in the example we are in the `repos` folder. If we want to get back to the folder inside `repos` called `digital-history`, we would type:

```
cd digital-history
```

Typing folder names can be cumbersome. But the command line has an enormous time-saver that you should get into the habit of using: tab completion. If you hit the tab key at any point, the command line will try to complete your command. For example, there is only one subfolder beginning with m in our `repos` folder, so within that folder we only really needed to type:

```
cd m
```

and hit tab and return. If you are trying this out yourself, which we hope you are, you will of course need to have a subfolder beginning with the right letter for anything to be completed. Tab completion works in many scenarios and is particularly useful with long file and directory names.

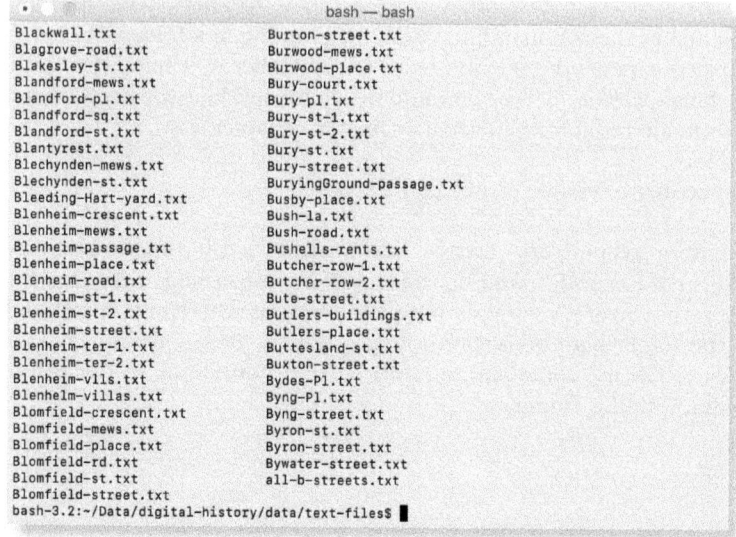

Figure 4.7 Folder contents shown by ls

Finally, we want to see what is available in our working folder: what files and folders are there? For this we use the command ls. If you type ls ('list' was obviously considered too verbose for this command) inside any folder, you get a list of files and subfolders.

> **Getting out of trouble**
> If you do not type a complete command, the command line may give you a flashing cursor, but you cannot type anything, or a new line with an indented cursor (it is expecting a multi-line command).
>
> In these cases, pressing the control key and the c key at the same time should solve the problem.

Before moving on you might like to practise navigating around your file system from the command line. If it helps, to start with you could put your normal, graphical way of navigating (such as Windows Explorer) next to your command line window to help you see where you are and where you want to go. As you become more confident you can dispense with this and just navigate with cd, pwd and ls.

GREP

After our excursus, let us return to our questions about address patterns in the directories. For this we need one particular, extremely useful tool that the command line offers: `grep`. Grep originally stood for 'global regular expression print', but it is never referred to in full, so it is technically an anacronym – that is, an acronym whose expansion is mostly forgotten.

`Grep` is probably the single most useful command for a historian to learn. It searches through a file, or files, and returns only those lines that contain what was searched for. As is often the case with the command line, this command is simple in itself and its power comes through combining it with other commands.

Have your command line window open and be sure that you have navigated to the folder containing the text files of the Post Office directories that you downloaded earlier. If you have trouble navigating manually with `cd`, you can always use the Windows and Mac tips given above. If you type `pwd` now, you should see a file path ending in `data/text-files`.

At the prompt, enter the following:

```
grep "1" Balls-pond-road.txt
```

Did you remember to use tab completion? You only really need to type

```
grep "1" Balls
```

followed by a tab. After pressing enter, you should see something like the screen shown in Figure 4.8.

You will see that the prompt is immediately ready for the next command. This is the end of the results returned (`grep` is very fast and you may not have even seen the first results flash past). By default, `grep` prints entire lines, in this case any line containing the digit 1.

Our regular expression for finding numbers at the beginning of a line was `^[0-9]+`. Let's try that with `grep`:

```
grep "^[0-9]+"
```

You should see no results. `Grep` searches for literal strings by default. We need to do the equivalent of ticking the regex box, as we did in a text

```
bash-3.2:~/Data/digital-history/data/text-files$ grep "1" Balls-Pond-road.txt
1 Clarke John, baker
11 Stokes Nathaniel, hosier
13 Mitchell Miss Elizh. confectioner
15 Webb Frederick, butcher
17 Langton Joseph, clothes dealer
19 Rust Mrs. Jane, wine merchant
21 Chambers George, tailor
39 & 41 Jolly Charles Young, beer retailer
51 Dupont George, tailor
61 Geyton Charles Abbott, grainer
81 Lickfold William, greengrocer
101 Mitchell Jas. & Co. loan office
105 Pettit George, watchmaker
113 Miller James, carpenter
115 Dyson William, gasfitter
117 Manton Matthew, baker
119 Duke of Wellington, George Henry Bambridge
121 Gray William Charles
123 Wells Joseph John
127 Bressey Mrs
133 Sims & Dupont, costume mnfrs
137 Smith Charles
139 Harewood Mrs
141 Ewins Daniel John
143 Wilbraham Miss U. ladies' schl
147 Trewinard Benjamin
151 Rowley George
155 Parker Mrs
161 Pearce Mrs
```

```
12 Root Joseph, greengrocer
14 Crank Charles, dairyman
16 & 26 Rix John, hairdresser
26 & 16 Rix John, hairdresser
100 Warren George, hair manufctr
102 Allen Alfred, coffee rooms
104 Docwra Thos. & Son, contractrs
106 Fryer Thomas Nickells
108 Colston James
110 Thompson Mrs
112 Buttifant George
114 Marsh William. linendraper
116 Mainwaring Richd. tobacconist
118 Turner Edward Anstee, chemist
120 Mildmay tavern, Thos. Flowers
122 Bibbye Wm. & Alfred, shoema
124 CrowsonIsaac&Son,cheese fctrs
126 Strapp George, corn dealer
130 Davis John, confectioner
132 Thain Hy. John, leather seller
134 LeGrand Mrs. Marion, milliner
134A, Cole Fredk. Wm. cabinet ma
136 Lawrence Jhn. pictr. frame ma
138 Lewis Ansell, bootmaker
140 White Edward & Co. grocer
146 Ball's Pond Branch Dispensary
160 Garrett Saml. Chas. watchmkr
164 Bradford Frdk. house decorator
166 Ball's Pond Brewery Co
bash-3.2:~/Data/digital-history/data/text-files$
```

Figures 4.8a-b The results of `grep "1" Balls-Pond-road.txt` editor. On the command line the equivalent is a 'flag' – in this case -E, placed immediately after the command:

```
grep -E "^[0-9]+" Balls-pond-road.txt
```

This may not immediately seem very useful. But now that we have this list of lines, we can do other things with it. We can further search it, we can count things within it, we can sort it. A key point in understanding the usefulness of the command line is that very often we want to make lists from other lists. This is exactly the kind of thing we do all the time when we search digital resources online. When you use an advanced search form and apply filters, you are making a list of search results from the list of the entire collection. The command line makes this searching and filtering process easy, fast and flexible, and works directly with the lines of text from within your files.

One of our questions is about coverage of addresses. How many addresses are there in comparison to potential addresses? As we said, this might tell us how well sampled the street was. With our data we can count using our regex and another flag to grep, this time -c. This returns a *count* of the lines that contain the regex and not the lines themselves:

```
grep -Ec "^[0-9]+" Balls-pond-road.txt
```

The command line should give the result:

```
164
```

This, of course, counts addresses made up of numbers, but it remains a helpful first approximation. Now we need the highest house number to see what the sampling ratio was, roughly speaking. When we ran our grep search without the counting flag, the last addresses were:

```
grep -E "^[0-9]+" Balls-Pond-road.txt
140
146
160
164
166
```

Seems suspicious. There are no odd numbers and there are fewer total numbered addresses (164) than the highest number (166). It looks like the even-numbered part of Balls Pond Road is listed last.

Without looking through the entire list, how can we have a look at the odd numbers? If you are now thinking, 'well, why not just look through the list?', the answer is that we want all of our methods to be extensible to very large datasets, with thousands or millions of results. So we want grep to look through the list for us.

One approach we can take is to modify our regex just a little bit so it only prints the odd numbers. Recall that the character class, the stuff inside square brackets, gives the only allowable options, so we can simply put odd numbers into it. At this point we might find that grep printing out the rest of the address line becomes distracting, so let us add one more flag, -o, which tells grep to print *only* the match, not the whole line:

```
grep -Eo "^[13579]+" Balls-pond-road.txt
```

But this gives us only strings of entirely odd digits, as you will see if you try it. We actually want any digits (or none) followed by a final odd digit. We need to break down the number search into two parts:

```
grep -Eo "^[0-9]*[13579] " Balls-pond-road.txt
```

This regex is getting complicated, but do not be put off: beyond a certain length they become difficult to read for everyone. The best way to understand this one is to make small changes and run it to see the differences. The best way to write complex regexes from scratch is to build them up incrementally rather than to write the whole thing in one go.

You will notice in the last regex that there is a space before the closing quotation marks. Can you see why? The difference is subtle, but without the space we would match the *beginning* of numbers like 138. Without the space, the digits 1 and 3 together match the criteria of being zero or more numbers from 0 to 9 (one of them in this case) followed by one odd number. The 8 is not matched and grep will return 13 as one of the results. Requiring a space ensures that this does not happen.

Why do we use * and not +? This is because we want all the odd numbers, including single-digit ones like 7. Using + would mean 'at least one digit' before the odd digit, and that would give us results like 17 but not 7. The * means 'any number of digits, including zero', and editor. On the command line the equivalent is a 'flag' – in this case -E, placed immediately after the command:

```
grep -E "^[0-9]+" Balls-pond-road.txt
```

This may not immediately seem very useful. But now that we have this list of lines, we can do other things with it. We can further search it, we can count things within it, we can sort it. A key point in understanding the usefulness of the command line is that very often we want to make lists from other lists. This is exactly the kind of thing we do all the time when we search digital resources online. When you use an advanced search form and apply filters, you are making a list of search results from the list of the entire collection. The command line makes this searching and filtering process easy, fast and flexible, and works directly with the lines of text from within your files.

One of our questions is about coverage of addresses. How many addresses are there in comparison to potential addresses? As we said, this might tell us how well sampled the street was. With our data we can count using our regex and another flag to grep, this time -c. This returns a *count* of the lines that contain the regex and not the lines themselves:

```
grep -Ec "^[0-9]+" Balls-pond-road.txt
```

The command line should give the result:

```
164
```

This, of course, counts addresses made up of numbers, but it remains a helpful first approximation. Now we need the highest house number to see what the sampling ratio was, roughly speaking. When we ran our grep search without the counting flag, the last addresses were:

```
grep -E "^[0-9]+" Balls-Pond-road.txt
140
146
160
164
166
```

Seems suspicious. There are no odd numbers and there are fewer total numbered addresses (164) than the highest number (166). It looks like the even-numbered part of Balls Pond Road is listed last.

Without looking through the entire list, how can we have a look at the odd numbers? If you are now thinking, 'well, why not just look through the list?', the answer is that we want all of our methods to be extensible to very large datasets, with thousands or millions of results. So we want grep to look through the list for us.

One approach we can take is to modify our regex just a little bit so it only prints the odd numbers. Recall that the character class, the stuff inside square brackets, gives the only allowable options, so we can simply put odd numbers into it. At this point we might find that grep printing out the rest of the address line becomes distracting, so let us add one more flag, -o, which tells grep to print *only* the match, not the whole line:

```
grep -Eo "^[13579]+" Balls-pond-road.txt
```

But this gives us only strings of entirely odd digits, as you will see if you try it. We actually want any digits (or none) followed by a final odd digit. We need to break down the number search into two parts:

```
grep -Eo "^[0-9]*[13579] " Balls-pond-road.txt
```

This regex is getting complicated, but do not be put off: beyond a certain length they become difficult to read for everyone. The best way to understand this one is to make small changes and run it to see the differences. The best way to write complex regexes from scratch is to build them up incrementally rather than to write the whole thing in one go.

You will notice in the last regex that there is a space before the closing quotation marks. Can you see why? The difference is subtle, but without the space we would match the *beginning* of numbers like 138. Without the space, the digits 1 and 3 together match the criteria of being zero or more numbers from 0 to 9 (one of them in this case) followed by one odd number. The 8 is not matched and grep will return 13 as one of the results. Requiring a space ensures that this does not happen.

Why do we use * and not +? This is because we want all the odd numbers, including single-digit ones like 7. Using + would mean 'at least one digit' before the odd digit, and that would give us results like 17 but not 7. The * means 'any number of digits, including zero', and

WORKING WITH TEXT 1: UNSTRUCTURED TEXT 79

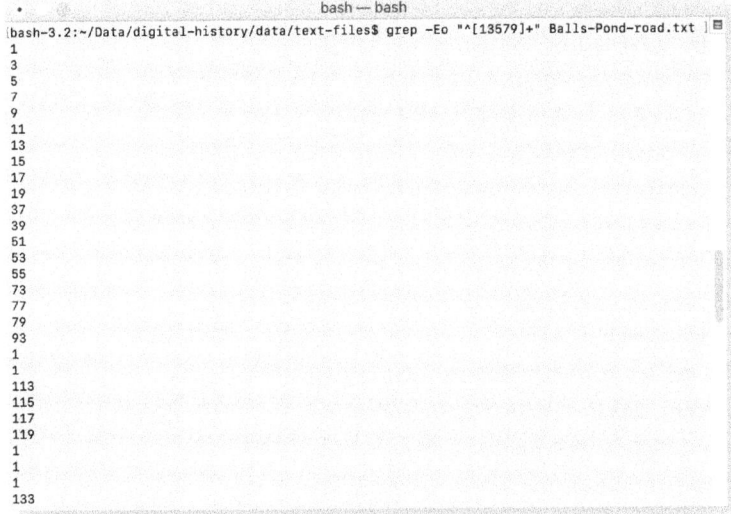

Figure 4.9 The results of grep -Eo "^[13579]+" Balls-Pond-road.txt

80 DOING DIGITAL HISTORY

```
[bash-3.2:~/Data/digital-history/data/text-files$ grep -Eo "^[0-9]*[13579] " Balls-Pond-road.txt
1
3
5
7
9
11
13
15
17
19
21
23
25
27
29
37
39
43
47
49
51
53
55
61
73
77
79
81
```

```
201
203
205
207
209
211
215
217
219
221
225
227
229
231
233
235
237
239
241
243
245
249
251
253
255
257
259
261
261
bash-3.2:~/Data/digital-history/data/text-files$
```

Figures 4.10a-b The results of grep -Eo "^[0-9]*[13579] " Balls-Pond-road.txt

Table 4.3 The most useful grep flags

Flag	Effect
-i	case insensitive
-h	suppress the file name
-c	give a count of results
-n	print the line number
-E	use regex
-v	show lines that *do not* match
-r	also search files in sub folders
-o	only show the search string

so does what we want here. Try swapping + and * to see the different results produced.

We have now introduced a number of flags that can alter the behaviour of grep. Actually, we have told you most of the really important ones. Table 4.3 contains a list of all the most useful grep flags for reference. We really encourage you to try these out and combine them, especially on your own data.

Given what you now know, you can try using two separate greps to print out the number of odd and the number of even address strings in Balls-Pond-road.txt.[8] For us, this resulted in ninety-one odd and seventy-two even addresses being found. Without knowing anything else, this already suggests a lack of consistency in our data. Was this just chance?

We need to look in more detail at the results, to see if there are any differences in the better-represented odd numbers and the even numbers. We could write the results to a couple of files in the same folder so that we can look at them in a text editor of choice. This is how you write the results of a grep, or any other command, to a new file:

```
grep  -E   "^[0-9]*[13579] "  Balls-pond-road.txt  >
odds.txt
grep  -E   "^[0-9]*[02468] "  Balls-pond-road.txt  >
evens.txt
```

The angle bracket > sends the result of the grep not to the screen but to a file, which is created by the command. *Note that if a file with that name already exists it will be overwritten.*

CONNECTING COMMANDS WITH PIPES

We have been saying that the power of the command line lies in stringing together simple commands, and it is time to show how that works. You are now reasonably familiar with grep. It really does not do very much more, on its own, than the things we have been working through.

But you can also page through the results on screen. To do this we need to send the results of the grep program to another program, called less, which allows you to scroll back and forth. We do this with the pipe symbol (|). This method is powerful and we will use it more shortly. For now, try this:

```
grep  -E  "^[0-9]*[13579]  "  Balls-pond-road.txt   |
less
```

When we produced results with grep previously, it went straight through to the last results that could fit on the screen. The less program, by contrast, shows the results of grep a screenful at a time. Use the arrow keys to go up and down the results. To quit and go back to a prompt, press 'q' and try the same thing with:

```
grep  -E  "^[0-9]*[02468]  "  Balls-pond-road.txt   |
less
```

As we scroll through the results, it seems as if the odd numbers have more addresses which are private houses, because there is no profession ascribed to the occupant. For example:

```
171 Hinley Mrs
```

compared with:

```
173 Holloway Frederick, auctioneer
```

It looks as if it is a characteristic of private addresses that they do not have a comma anywhere in the line. This is an incredibly simple pattern, and not universally true, as you will see from address number 60 if you are following along with the searches yourself, but we can still use it to compare the number of private addresses and business addresses.

WORKING WITH TEXT 1: UNSTRUCTURED TEXT 83

Figure 4.11 The results of grep -Eo "^[0-9]*[13579] " Balls-Pond-road.txt | less

If you look back to the box that lists the flags to grep, you will see that there is one flag that returns lines that do not contain the search pattern: -v. For example, we can find all the lines in a file which do not contain any numbers at all with:

   grep -v "[0-9]" Balls-pond-road.txt

We are going to use the -v flag to help us filter and count at the same time. We can filter grep results by piping grep to a second grep command. Try this first:

   grep -E "^[0-9]*[13579]+ " Balls-pond-road.txt | grep ","

(these results are the commercial properties on the odd side of the road)

   grep -E "^[0-9]*[13579]+ " Balls-pond-road.txt | grep -v ","

(these are mainly non-commercial properties on the odd side of the road).

To be clear, the second grep in each of these commands is not searching the file. It is searching only the results of the first grep. To visualise what is going on, think of the process of first writing the results to a new file and then running a separate search of that new file. We could do that with this sequence of commands:

```
grep -E "^[0-9]*[13579] " Balls-pond-road.txt > newfile.txt
```

then

```
grep "," newfile.txt
```

Pipes allows us to dispense with the intermediate files, such as newfile.txt, and manipulate each set of results with each additional pipe we choose to add. We only want the final result, after all, so using pipes is much faster.

It can be hard to see in your mind's eye what is going on with a sequence of pipes. If you are unclear at any stage, you can either show the intermediate results on the screen or send them to a file to see exactly what they contain. With practice, it becomes easier to keep each part of the sequence mentally distinct.

We displayed results above rather than count them so as to be very clear about what is happening. Now we are confident that we are filtering correctly, we can count instead:

```
grep -E "^[0-9]*[13579] " Balls-pond-road.txt |
grep -c ","
grep -E "^[0-9]*[13579] " Balls-pond-road.txt |
grep -cv ","
grep -E "^[0-9]*[02468] " Balls-pond-road.txt |
grep -c ","
grep -E "^[0-9]*[02468] " Balls-pond-road.txt |
grep -cv ","
```

Notice that the -c flag is on the second grep, not the first. Can you see why? If not, try breaking down the commands without using a pipe to strengthen your mental model of what is happening with each grep. The results we get are shown in table 4.4.

When displayed like this, it looks to us as if there are not proportionately more residential properties on one side of the street after

Table 4.4 Grep results for commercial and residential properties

	Commercial	Residential
Odd numbers	60	31
Even numbers	50	22

all. But we may have discovered a fast way to count residential and non-residential properties across the entire corpus. These commercial properties may have residents, of course, but we think we are justified in regarding them as different in kind from purely residential properties. Even if there is noise in the data which means we cannot generate flawless lists of the two property types, across a corpus we may be able to find predominantly commercial and predominantly residential roads. We will come back to searching all the files, instead of just the one for Balls Pond Road, at the end of the chapter.

Up to now we have been counting addresses that only contain numbers. If we are working at sufficient scale, we might decide that this is an acceptable simplification, or we might not. As we are looking at one street, let us go beyond numbers.

Can you think of a way to list and count addresses which do not contain numbers? In other words, to get a result like in Figure 4.12? Think back to our first regex, to find the numbers at the beginning of the line. Initially we want the opposite of that, which we can do by adding the -v flag:

```
grep -Ev "^[0-9]+" Balls-pond-road.txt
```

The results show up quite a lot of noise. This is quite normal with grep. Remember that we can filter out the cross streets, marked in the text with 'here is' and the north and south side headers with further greps:

```
grep -Ev "^[0-9]+" Balls-pond-road.txt | grep -v "here is" | grep -v "SIDE"
```

and we can do further cleaning up if we want to, eliminating one more pattern of noise with each additional grep:

```
grep -Ev "^[0-9]+" Balls-pond-road.txt | grep -v "here is" | grep -v "SIDE" | grep -v "MAP" | grep -v "Ball's Pond"
```

```
[bash-3.2:~/Data/digital-history/data/text-files$
Ball's Pond road (N.),
Essex road, Islington, to Kingsland road.
MAP O4, O5, P5.
SOUTH SIDE.
Gadsby William
CONGREGATIONAL CHAPEL
here is Culford road
here is Southgate road
Butt Frederick, shopkeeper
Mosedale Jas. veterinary surgn
here is Cross street
NORTH SIDE.
Eldridge George, machinist
here is Stanley road
here is Canterbury road
here is Kingsbury road
CUTLERS' ALMSHOUSES
 METROPOLITAN BENEFIT SOCIETY'S ASYLUM, Henry Patient sec
BOOKBINDERS' PROVIDENT INSTITUTION, J. Jeffrey, sec
here is King Henry's walk
here is Mildmay park
West David Ormond, surgeon
bash-3.2:~/Data/digital-history/data/text-files$
```

Figure 4.12 The results of grep -Ev "^[0-9]+" Balls-Pond-road.txt

As in Figure 4.12, this leaves us with nine additional properties for possible investigation.

Let us now move on from one road to all the roads in our sample. We have 591 roads in total, each in a file of its own. To operate across all of them at once with grep, instead of an explicit filename we can use * as a wildcard, meaning 'any characters at this point in the filename'. So *.txt means 'any file in the folder ending in .txt':

    grep -E "^[0-9]" *.txt

This gives us a lot of results, so we will use less again so we can page up and down using the arrow keys:

    grep -E "^[0-9]" *.txt | less

Notice that, by default, when you search more than one file, grep prints the filename followed by the result in that file. This means that we can see that some streets really do seem to be primarily residential, such as Balfour Road. Others, like Back Church Lane, are mostly commercial.

```
Baches-st.txt:10 Ghurney Richd. french polisher
Baches-st.txt:9 Walker Edwd. boot & shoe makr
Baches-st.txt:15 Morgan Thos.Jsph.who.shoe mkr
Back-Church-lane.txt:11 & 13 Wells Wm. Thos. rag mer
Back-Church-lane.txt:45 Mullins Thomas Trigbuth
Back-Church-lane.txt:51 Palmer Chas. S. chandler's shop
Back-Church-lane.txt:65 BrinjesJ.F.animl.charcl.re-burnr
Back-Church-lane.txt:77 Burrows John & Co. grocers
Back-Church-lane.txt:87 Wilson John Wm. bootmaker
Back-Church-lane.txt:123 & 125 StanleyJhn. furniture dlr
Back-Church-lane.txt:129 Powell Thos. boot & shoe makr
Back-Church-lane.txt:131 Herwig Geo. Jhn.chandler's shp
Back-Church-lane.txt:32 Cuthbert Wm.& G. brassfounders
Back-Church-lane.txt:74 Nosworthy Ths. chandler's shop
Back-Church-lane.txt:132 Hammant Thos. Jhn. hairdrssr
Back-hill.txt:7 to 12 SnewinChas.B.N.tmbr.mer
Back-hill.txt:16 Burnham Richd. cabinet turner
Backs-row.txt:1 Murrell Wm. Chas.coal mer
Backs-row.txt:3 & 15 Abbott Mary & Co. coal merchants
Backs-row.txt:8 Girling J. & H. coal merchts
Backs-row.txt:9 & 10 Warren Frederio & Co. coal merchants
Backs-row.txt:14 ParryThs. S.& Chs. coal mer
Backs-row.txt:15 & 3 Abbott Mrs. Mary & Co. coal merchants
Backs-row.txt:16 Mitchell Joseph & Co. coal merchants
Backs-row.txt:17 Thornicroft & Co. coal mers
Bagshot-street.txt:47 Cooper Miss E. B. haberdasher
Bagshot-street.txt:39 Rattenbury Mrs.Elizh.wardrb.dlr
Baker-st.txt:1 Drew Thos. Wm. chandlr.'s shop
Baker-st.txt:18 Winterton Andrw.chandler's shp
:
```

Figure 4.13 The results of `grep -E "^[0-9]" *.txt | grep -v "," | less`

As you page through, you might notice quite a few commercial properties that do not have that diagnostic comma that we thought we might be able to use. We can check by filtering out the lines with a comma – that is, by piping to `grep -v`:

`grep -E "^[0-9]" *.txt | grep -v "," | less`

This clarifies things. The comma is often missing. Perhaps it is especially likely be omitted when lines are long and the typesetters needed to save space.

We are now face to face with the problem of messy data. It seems that the comma *may* reliably point to commercial properties, but the absence is not so reliable. In this chapter we have been looking at unstructured data and we are now seeing that it has its limitations. In the next chapter we will discuss structured data and how to explore it.

TEST YOURSELF

To test your knowledge of the techniques in this chapter, try answering the following questions using grep and regex:

1. Are there any subdivided properties, as indicated by having letters after their numbers, in Ball's Pond Road? Hint: in your regex you will need a character class that we have mentioned but not yet explicitly used.
2. If we try to find the highest number in each file by using *.txt to grep through them all, we will hit a problem quite quickly because of the way that pipes work. Can you see what that problem is? If you are not sure then experimenting may make things clearer.
3. We have not yet properly investigated addresses without a number. We might imagine that this could happen with very grand buildings or with very marginal back streets with no official numbering. Can you call up all the unnumbered lines from all the files and page through them? What ways can you find to filter out cross streets and other noise?

You have now used most of the tools that regex and grep offer. More complexity can be built up with pipes, and we will discuss some more commands in the next chapter, but the way to internalise and become proficient with the possibilities is to practise. Try now to devise some historical questions of your own about the plain text files we have made available and then attempt to investigate the data using grep and regex.

NOTES

1 Barney, *The Etymologies of Isidore of Seville*, I.xli.
2 Hitchcock, 'Confronting the Digital', 19.
3 Atkins, *The Directories of London: 1677–1977*, p. 124ff.
4 Atkins, *The Directories of London: 1677–1977*.
5 Note that a few text editors use \(and \) to mark capture groups, and \1 instead of $1 for recalling them, but this is less common.
6 A note on terminology: we are using 'command line' in this book, but elsewhere you will also see synonyms like 'shell' or 'terminal'. The

command line itself runs a default program, normally one called Bash, so you will sometimes see 'Bash' used as a synonym as well. A web search can usually find instructions for anything you want to do on the command line, but be aware that these various terms might be used instead of 'command line'.

7 When you open a very large file in a text editor, the program has to load the whole thing into memory at once, which limits the size of files that can be accommodated. Most command line programs only have one line at a time in memory, which means that they can process enormous files, even if it takes a while.

8 `grep -Ec "^[0-9]*[13579] " Balls-pond-road-txt` and `grep -Ec "^[0-9]*[02468] " Balls-pond-road-txt`.

↠ 5 ↞

WORKING WITH TEXT 2: STRUCTURED TEXT

In the last chapter we had a close look at a transcription of Balls Pond Road in an *unstructured* format. We were able to differentiate some features of the text with regular expressions, but things like cross streets and map references added noise to the data that was cumbersome to deal with. In this chapter we will explore the same data *structured* in the format XML and see what advantages that brings, and what difficulties remain.

As a historian, the format of structured data you are likeliest to come across is XML, because it is well suited to continuous text. XML, then, is what we will focus on in this chapter. There are two other common formats which we touched on in Chapter 2, CSV and JSON. Working with JSON is beyond the scope of this book, but CSV lends itself well to the command line techniques we have already covered. We use CSV (and the similar TSV) in Chapter 7. In our command line recipes list in Appendix 2 we show how you can extract a particular column from a CSV file using the command cut.

XML is easier to work with than to create from scratch, so we will begin by using XML versions of our Post Office directory data. At the end of the chapter we will give you an overview of what to consider when marking up text in your own bespoke XML.

Text editors are a useful tool for viewing XML files and making minor changes. We will return to this topic later when discussing how you can write your own XML, where a dedicated XML editor makes things much easier.

When we worked with Balls Pond Road in an unstructured format, the main things we had to work with were line beginnings and endings and the presence or absence of a comma. Structured data such as XML gives us more options and we will see if we can use it to look at questions like:

- Can we list professions by frequency?
- Can we sort female professions by married status?
- Do women live in longer streets? What would this mean?
- Do women live in more professional or more domestic streets?

Please now open Balls-Pond-road.xml, which you can find in the XML folder in the repository, in your text editor. Here is the beginning of the file:

```
<street>
<head>Ball's Pond road (N.),</head><head2><i>Essex
road, Islington, to Kingsland road</i>.</head2>
<map>MAP O4, O5, P5.</map>
<side>SOUTH SIDE.</side>
<addr>1 Clarke John, baker</addr>
<addr>3 Alder Charles, umbrella maker</addr>
<addr>5 Hide George, haberdasher</addr>
```

What was previously plain text is now 'marked up' by having sets of angle brackets wrapped around it. Each address is marked up in the same way:

```
<addr>1 Clarke John, Baker</addr>
```

<addr> is the opening tag and </addr> is the closing tag (together they are known as an element). You will notice that they are the same, except the closing tag has a forward slash after the opening angle bracket. XML does not prescribe element names: we invented the name addr as a suitable one to mark up this particular document. XML elements like this must have matching opening and closing tags. Note also that tags are case sensitive, so <addr> and </Addr> cannot form an element.

For now, the only other rules of XML we will mention are that complete elements must be fully inside each other, like Russian dolls, and not overlapping. If you look at the very top and bottom of the file Balls-Pond-road.xml, you will see that all other elements are contained, or 'nested', within the street element – that is, everything else comes between in between:

```
<street>
```
all other XML
```
</street>
```

This element, in this case `street`, is known as the 'root element', and every XML file must have one.

An important part of XML is that what is marked up is often *what it means*, rather than its typographical function. The markup is semantic. For example, the `addr` element was chosen by us to mark up addresses, based on our understanding that these are actually addresses. At the end of the chapter, to show the flexibility of XML, we will ask you to choose some other semantic features to mark up, and to invent your own element names with which to do so.

With the addresses all marked up in our text, we can ask more questions than we could with unstructured text, and because XML is a plain text format we can still use our old tool, `grep`.

FEMALE PROFESSIONS

Now that we can reliably extract addresses, because they are marked up, we can begin to look at the gender of listed occupants. As noted when we introduced the directory in Chapter 3, women are given titles, mostly Miss and Mrs, but men are usually not. We can use this to, for example, look at ratios of men to women in different streets. We may even be able to look at professions by gender. We said in the last chapter that counting, filtering and sorting were – boring as they may sound – at the heart of effective search and can often illuminate interesting patterns in the data. At the end of this chapter we will use those tools to list the most common professions for women and men in our data.

Can we first verify that men are not given titles? The first thing we can do is search for 'Mr' from the command line. Be sure that your command line is opened in the XML folder now (for instructions on how to navigate, see Chapter 4). Type the following:

```
grep "Mr" *.xml
```

We are just using the default `grep` here, which returns the whole line and allows us to see that the results are generally giving us the word 'Mrs'. We can exclude those with `grep -v`:

```
grep "Mr" *.xml | grep -v "Mrs"
```

WORKING WITH TEXT 2: STRUCTURED TEXT

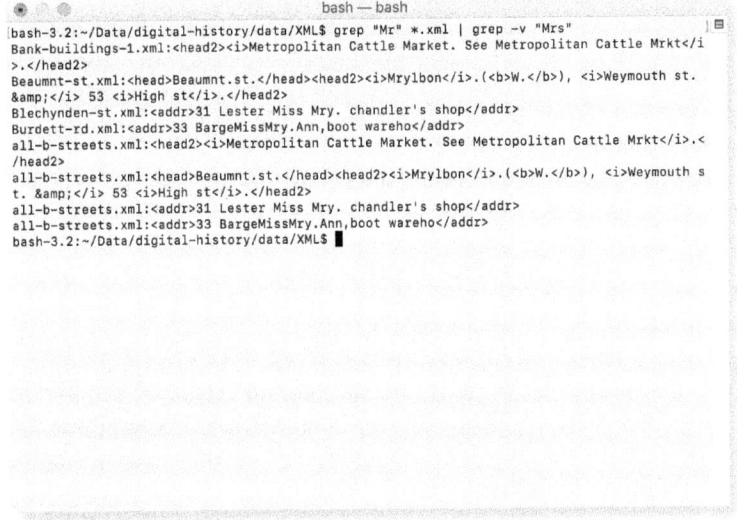

Figure 5.1 The results of grep "Mr" *.xml | grep -v "Mrs"

Our remaining results seem to be abbreviations of 'Mary', presumably for space reasons in the directory.

What about other male titles? To make this search easier, we have included in the folder a file called all-b-streets.xml, which you will have seen cropping up in search results.[1] We can search just this file for 'Sir' like this:

```
grep "Sir" all-b-streets.xml
```

There are some Sirs, and if you count them with grep -c you will see forty results. Can we simply discount forty results in this data set? Now that we have the data in XML, we can count all addresses to get a sense of the base rate:

```
grep -c "<addr>" all-b-streets.xml
```

There are 14,021 addresses, so the Sirs are 0.29% of the total, which we think means the occurrence of 'Sir' in this data can be discounted. Not surprisingly, none of them have a profession, such as 'butcher', listed either, so if we want to use titles to find professions by gender, they are unlikely to interfere with our results. We may, though, have found a useful way to pick out the most prosperous streets in our sample. The results for 'Lord' are messier because this can be a surname as well as a title. We invite you to look through these results, although we think they can be discounted too.

We can count addresses listing the string 'Mrs' or 'Miss' very easily:

```
grep -c "Mrs" all-b-streets.xml
grep -c "Miss" all-b-streets.xml
```

Recall that what is returned here is the sequence of characters that make up 'Mrs' or 'Miss', not the words themselves. This can give us some unwanted results. For example, if you `grep` for 'Mission', you will see some results: these would also appear in our `grep` for 'Miss' above and give us a false count. If you cannot quite see how this works, again it is best to explore with `grep`:

```
grep "Mission" all-b-streets.xml
```

then

```
grep "Mission" all-b-streets.xml | grep "Miss"
```

You will see the same results both times.

We can try to account for this with a complicated regex but, fortunately, `grep` makes it easy for us to match a complete word: we can use \b for a word boundary. Word boundary means any one of a space, a punctuation mark, or the beginning or end of a line.

```
grep -Ec "\bMrs\b" all-b-streets.xml
grep -Ec "\bMiss\b" all-b-streets.xml
```

The effect of using \b is that we are searching for 'Mrs' and 'Miss' as individual words, so 'Mission', for example, will no longer be matched. As we are now using regex, we need the -E flag, or the search would be for a literal \b.

The results for these are 1,129 and 342, respectively, so we can see immediately that married (or widowed) women are roughly three times as frequently listed as occupants than unmarried women.

Unfortunately, there is no easy way for us to find all of the female titles that may be in the data. This is because the data is not marked up to that level of detail. We know that there are 14,021 addresses, so it would be a good couple of days' work for an interested researcher to mark up all of the titles, female and male. We will come back to this example at the end of the chapter when we discuss adding your own XML to documents.

Because `grep` is very fast, we can fire off some searches in `all-b-streets.xml` and find things like Misses (42), Madame (26) and Duchess (3). It seems to us that these are small quantities of unusual titles which roughly equal the unusual male titles like Sir. We are taking a broad overview of the data here and so will ignore these unusual titles.

To answer our question about the approximate ratio of listed men to listed women, we want to combine a search for 'Mrs' or 'Miss', which we can do in regex with a pipe: |. Note that | in regex has a different meaning from | when it pipes one command to another on the command line! Because we are using regex, we will also need to use the -E flag:

```
grep -Ec "\bMrs\b|\bMiss\b" all-b-streets.xml
```

This gives us 1,465 results. Can you see why we do not in fact get the sum of 1,129 and 342, which we found in our individual searches above?

It is important to remember that `grep` returns lines which contain the result, and it is lines which are being counted here. A few lines in our data contain both 'Mrs' and 'Miss', and this accounts for the discrepancy: they only get counted once when we combine the searches. To verify this, you can `grep` for one term and then `grep` the results for the other term:

```
grep -E "\bMiss\b" all-b-streets.xml | grep -E "\bMrs\b"
```

Despite our caveats about noise in the data, we can now find the approximate ratio of men and women listed as occupants. We get the men by counting addresses which do not contain the words 'Miss' or 'Mrs':

```
grep "<addr>" all-b-streets.xml | grep -Evc "\bMrs\b|\bMiss\b"
```

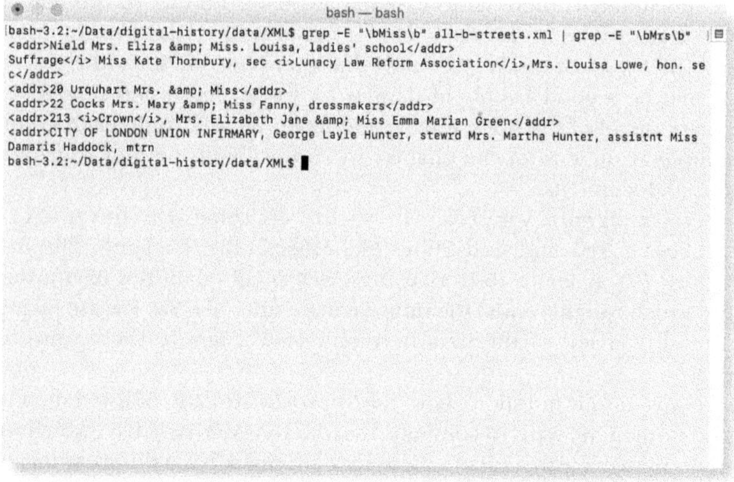

```
bash-3.2:~/Data/digital-history/data/XML$ grep -E "\bMiss\b" all-b-streets.xml | grep -E "\bMrs\b"
<addr>Nield Mrs. Eliza &amp; Miss. Louisa, ladies' school</addr>
Suffrage</i> Miss Kate Thornbury, sec <i>Lunacy Law Reform Association</i>,Mrs. Louisa Lowe, hon. sec</addr>
<addr>20 Urquhart Mrs. &amp; Miss</addr>
<addr>22 Cocks Mrs. Mary &amp; Miss Fanny, dressmakers</addr>
<addr>213 <i>Crown</i>, Mrs. Elizabeth Jane &amp; Miss Emma Marian Green</addr>
<addr>CITY OF LONDON UNION INFIRMARY, George Layle Hunter, stewrd Mrs. Martha Hunter, assistnt Miss Damaris Haddock, mtrn
bash-3.2:~/Data/digital-history/data/XML$
```

Figure 5.2 The results of grep -E "\bMiss\b" all-b-streets.xml | grep -E "\bMrs\b"

and the women by counting addresses which do contain those words:

```
grep "<addr>" all-b-streets.xml | grep -Ec "\bMrs\b|\bMiss\b"
```

Our ratio is 12,576:1,445, so about 11.5% of the occupants are listed as women. Now that we have a rough mean average, we can search the individual streets and find outliers with either high or low numbers of women. There is another caveat here, which is that institutions, such as churches and pubs, are being counted as male. Recall that what we are doing here is making initial overviews of the data so that we can decide where research effort might best be focused. In the 'Test yourself' section at the end of the chapter, we have included a question about how you could exclude those institutions if you thought it worthwhile.

We will finish this section by doing something a little more complicated: counting the individual professions for women and men and ordering the results by the most frequently occurring professions. To do this we will need two more very useful command line programs: sort and uniq.

This also brings together many of the `grep` commands we have been using. These are the steps we need:

1. Find all the addresses containing the words 'Miss' or 'Mrs'
2. From the results, extract the text after the last comma of the address (the occupation)
3. Sort the results
4. Count the unique results
5. Order the results numerically

We could run this on the complete file or all the individual streets together with only a minor variation of searching `*.xml` or `all-b-streets.xml`. Here we will use the latter, because the process is already complicated and using one file is a bit simpler. We have already covered Step 1:

```
grep "<addr>" all-b-streets.xml | grep -E
"\bMrs\b|\bMiss\b"
```

For our regex, we need to target the last comma in the line. To get this we need to introduce one last little bit of syntax. You remember that a character class is a set of individual characters, any of which can match. Its inverse is a character class where *none* of the characters are allowed to match. This allows us to ensure that a character or characters – in this case a comma – do not appear. In regex you put a caret at the beginning of the set of characters to say 'anything except one of these':

```
[^,]+
```

This means 'any number of characters that is not a comma'. Why do we want this? Because some addresses have multiple commas, such as

```
<addr>59A, M'Carty Mrs. Ann, haberdashr</addr>
```

in Brick Lane. We only want 'haberdashr' in our results. The full regex is:

```
,[^,]+</addr>
```

This means 'a comma, followed by anything not a comma, followed by a closing address tag'. It ensures we only get the last comma and whatever

```
, shirt maker</addr>
,boot wareho</addr>
, oil warehouse</addr>
, juvenile dressmaker</addr>
, dressmaker</addr>
, milliner</addr>
, haberdasher</addr>
, matron</addr>
, Mrs. Sarah Friend</addr>
, linendra</addr>
, dressmaker</addr>
, proprietor</addr>
, stay makr</addr>
, milliner</addr>
, jeweller</addr>
, perfmr</addr>
, dressmaker</addr>
,ladies' school</addr>
, lodging ho</addr>
, lodginghouse</addr>
, lodging house</addr>
, lodging ho</addr>
, vellum bindr</addr>
, chandler's shop</addr>
, coffee rms</addr>
, carman</addr>
, midwife</addr>
, midwife</addr>
, laundress</addr>
bash-3.2:~/Data/digital-history/data/XML$
```

Figure 5.3 The results of grep "<addr>" all-b-streets.xml | grep -E "\bMrs\b|\bMiss\b" | grep -Eo ",[^,]+</addr>"

comes after it. Try this search and you will see from the results how it works:

```
grep "<addr>" all-b-streets.xml | grep -E "\bMrs\
b|\bMiss\b" | grep -Eo ",[^,]+</addr>"
```

These are the female occupations but they are unsorted. To sort them, we can sort by piping to another program, one called sort:

```
grep "<addr>" all-b-streets.xml | grep -E "\bMrs\
b|\bMiss\b" | grep -Eo ",[^,]+</addr>" | sort
```

The default order is alphabetical. If you look through these results, you will see a few personal names, but these will not really disturb our results because each name will only occur once. More of a problem are the spelling variants.

You might think it worthwhile at this point to write the results out to a text file (we covered how to do this using > in the previous chapter), edit them into a more consistent form, and then do the final counts. We will leave this as an exercise for you if you would like to practise your skills.

The program `uniq` only returns lists items once: duplicates are dropped. With the flag `-c` it gives a count of how many duplicates were in the original list. This is extremely useful for counting from lists:

```
grep "<addr>" all-b-streets.xml | grep -E "\bMrs\
b|\bMiss\b" | grep -Eo ",[^,]+</addr>" | sort |
uniq -c
```

This gives us the information we wanted but it is still sorted alphabetically by profession.

We need to do one final sort, this time a numeric sort (otherwise 9 would appear after 11):

```
grep "<addr>" all-b-streets.xml | grep -E "\bMrs\
b|\bMiss\b" | grep -Eo ",[^,]+</addr>" | sort |
uniq -c | sort -n
   9 , baker</addr>
   9 , tobacconist</addr>
  13 , coffee rooms</addr>
  13 , lodging house</addr>
  18 , grocer</addr>
  23 , lodging ho</addr>
  24 , dressmaker</addr>
  29 , milliner</addr>
```

As we have said, this search is fairly complicated. It is a case where running each command yourself will make things clearer. Each individual part of it is easier to digest than the whole. We wanted to include this because this kind of sequence is a very fast way to count occurrences of things in all kinds of texts. We think that most historians would find a use for it, and after having used it a few times it will not appear so fearsome.

For the male professions, we only need to add one character, a `-v` flag, to the second `grep`.

```
grep "<addr>" all-b-streets.xml | grep -Ev "\bMrs\
b|\bMiss\b" | grep -Eo ",[^,]+</addr>" | sort |
uniq -c | sort -n
```

```
110 , butcher</addr>
118 , beer retailer</addr>
122 , greengrocer</addr>
123 , bootmaker</addr>
138 , solicitor</addr>
145 , grocer</addr>
151 , tailor</addr>
189 , baker</addr>
```

Our results have been suggestive and, when you have had some practice with the command line, very fast to generate, even with large amounts of text. But we do have to keep entering caveats that the markup does not allow us to analyse the text with any confidence. Therefore, in the next section we will discuss adding finer-grained tagging to existing XML files.

Now that you are practised at typing these commands, we will let you in on another time-saver when using the command line: you can use the up arrow to show your previous searches and then edit them. This makes modifying complex commands much easier, especially if you make a mistake.

ADDING YOUR OWN MARKUP

Let us look again at the first names in Ball's Pond Road:

```
<addr>1 Clarke John, baker</addr>
<addr>3 Alder Charles, umbrella maker</addr>
```

XML allows us to invent our own elements according to our own research interests. We could decide to mark up the occupations explicitly using an element we have decided to call occupation:

```
<addr>1 Clarke John, <occupation>baker</occupation>
</addr>
```

If we went through all of our data adding the occupation element, we would have a much more reliable set of occupations to work with. We could extract them all with a regex which would have more reliable results than relying on punctuation as we did above.

This is useful in itself, but if the focus of our research happened to be on the occupations in the Post Office directory then we would probably want to go further, categorising them in some way. The way to do this kind of thing in XML is to use what is known as an attribute, which gives a subcategory to an element.

Here we have chosen to use type as our attribute, and then we put a value in inverted commas. The values are whatever we want our types of occupation to be. In this example we have used the types 'foodstuffs' and 'crafts'. This would allow us to extract all of the craft-based occupations with grep or any other tool:

```
<addr>1 Clarke John, <occupation type="foodstuffs">
baker</occupation></addr>
<addr>3 Alder Charles, <occupation type="crafts">
umbrella maker</occupation></addr>
```

Because the attribute is not considered part of the element, the closing tag matches only the non-attribute part of the opening tag. You can see that this markup allows us to work either with the occupation elements as a whole or with a particular subset of them.

Multiple attributes are allowed. If we want to mark up the occupants with attributes relating to gender and marriage, then with Susan Hockridge's entry

```
<addr>9 HockridgeMrs.SusanAnn,bookslr</addr>
```

we could do something like this, using a person element with two attributes, gender and married:

```
<addr>9 <person gender="female"
married="yes">HockridgeMrs.SusanAnn</person>,
bookslr</addr>
```

This entry would not have been picked up by our grep for 'Mrs' with a word boundary. A full stop is a word boundary character but the letter e, of course, is not. However, if the files were marked up with attributes as above, we could find all of the married women with a simple grep and without the need for regex.

Why do we not add more elements instead of attributes? You might think of doing something like this:

```
<addr>9 <person><female>HockridgeMrs.SusanAnn</
female></person>,bookslr</addr>
```

This is entirely legitimate. However, our advice would be to avoid unwieldy markup by having no more than a few dozen elements in your XML and only one element per semantic unit. Here the element `female` will always mark up the same text as `person`, so we think a `gender` attribute is a better choice. But it is, as with everything in XML outside of the basic rules, the user's choice.

When we employed a keying company to transcribe part of the Post Office directory in XML, as outlined in Chapter 3, we were able to specify that addresses should be treated differently from other material. But it is important to know that the keyers work on the basis of things like typeface and page layout. They cannot be expected to interpret the meaning of any text they are asked to key. Professional keyers can only add semantic markup if it is also typographically identifiable in some way: they work on the basis of visual cues. So you can say '*every time text is underlined, capture it using the italic element*', but you cannot say '*capture all women's names using the female element*'. The art of writing good instructions is to be able to translate typographic features into meaningful chunks of data, as far as possible, and of not missing key elements in your text that you might later wish to use.

When you add your own XML you are likely to make mistakes. One of the rules for XML that we gave at the beginning of the chapter was: *nested elements must not overlap*. What this means is you cannot have:

```
<street><addr></street></addr>
```

If `<addr>` starts off being nested inside `<street>`, it has to finish inside it too, like this:

```
<street><addr></addr></street>
```

In large documents it is very difficult to keep track of nesting by eye. Nesting, in our experience, is the thing which most often goes awry when writing XML and is hardest to spot. We find the best approach is to open your document in a dedicated XML editor, which will immediately call your attention to things like incorrect nesting. These editors also offer many other aids to navigating and changing XML without making errors, and even understanding the structure of the overall document.

There are many XML editors available, and some of them are free, but on this occasion we would recommend the editor Oxygen (oxygenxml. com), which is not free but is very widely used and valued by digital historians.

Note that a text editor, like Sublime Text, is not an XML editor. An XML editor tries to understand the structure of the document when it opens the file, whereas a text editor treats it as just text. In practice this means that large XML documents can make XML editors run slowly, and very large files might crash the editor. If you are confident of the structure of your XML document, you may sometimes find it quicker to edit it in a dedicated text editor, especially for textual changes rather than changes to the structure of the XML.

Although you can invent elements, there are, as we have seen going along, a few fundamental rules of XML. To summarise:

1. Every file must have a root element
2. Elements must nest completely: no half-in, half-out stuff
3. Attribute values must be quoted, e.g. `married="yes"` or `married='yes'`, not `married=yes`

TEXT ENCODING INITIATIVE

Because you can mark up your XML texts in any way you choose, that means other people can too. The result is that if you gather together a set of texts from a number of different sources, you will have trouble using them as one collection. Someone may have marked up a paragraph using `<p>` or `<para>` or `<paragraph number="237">`. Just figuring out which uses which and mapping them to each other would be lot of work, and possibly prohibitive.

The TEI was designed to bring some order to potential chaos. TEI is a consortium that produces guidelines for how XML texts should be marked up. Of course, it has no authority over anybody and you can continue to invent your own XML elements as you please, but if you want to use your texts with other pre-encoded texts, or hope that others will use yours, then using TEI is a good idea. The first guidelines were produced in the late 1980s and have seen widespread adoption in the humanities.[2] A lot of thought and refinement has gone into the TEI guidelines over the years and they can inform your thinking about which elements and attributes to use, even if you modify TEI for your own XML.

For illustrative purposes, the XML text used for the Post Office directory digitised for this book is not TEI and is purely our own invention. TEI is more involved than the XML we have been using and it is probably best to feel confident with XML basics before moving on to working with TEI.

The guidelines do not lay down exactly how you should encode a particular piece of text: they are designed for researchers with very different interests and focuses. What they do is tell you that if you encode a paragraph you should use <p> and not <para> or <paragraph>. You might not care about marking up changes in typeface in your transcription, and you are quite free to leave this out of a TEI-compliant transcription, but if you do mark it up you should use <hi> (which stands for 'highlight') rather than, say, <i> or <emphasis>.

The full TEI guidelines cover most conceivable text types. They will tell you how to mark up the metre of a piece of verse or how a manuscript is bound. You do not have to read them all and probably few people have. For most purposes there is a cut-down version called TEI Lite, which is detailed enough for most XML encoding and is a good place to start with TEI.[3]

There are lots of good tools to help you with TEI available from their website (www.tei-c.org/), but you do not have to jump into learning TEI straight away. It is useful simply to be able to recognise a TEI-encoded text if you come across one. It will start with this line:

```
<TEI xmlns="http://www.tei-c.org/ns/1.0">
```

A TEI file should then have a `teiHeader` element, which encodes key metadata about the file, such as who was responsible for creating it.[4] Thereafter, if you are puzzled by any of the elements used, you can look them up in the published encoding guidelines. Everyone does this with TEI sometimes, including the authors of this book.

TEST YOURSELF

1. Find the most common professions of married and unmarried women from `all-b-streets.xml`
2. Choose your own elements to mark up one of the streets in the XML folder, within the three constraints of XML listed above
3. Extract your new elements from the file you altered using `grep`

NOTES

1. To combine many files into one, which is often a convenient thing to do, you can use the `cat` command: `cat *.xml > all-streets.txt`. We use a .txt extension here to avoid recursion. If we output `cat` to a file called `all-streets.xml`, this file would be created and then the command would apply to the new file too, because it also matches `*.xml`. The file would be added to itself. There are various ways around this, but using a different extension is perhaps simplest. You can then rename the file as `.xml`, which is what we have in the repository.
2. 'TEI: History', TEI, https://tei-c.org/about/history/ (accessed 28 June 2020).
3. 'TEI: TEI Lite', TEI, www.tei-c.org/guidelines/customization/lite/ (accessed 28 June 2020).
4. 'P5: Guidelines for electronic text encoding and interchange', TEI, www.tei-c.org/release/doc/tei-p5-doc/en/html/HD.html (accessed 28 June 2020).

⇶ 6 ⇷

CARING FOR YOUR DIGITAL HISTORY PROJECT

> Shifting from ink on paper to digital text suddenly allows us to make perfect copies of our work. Shifting from isolated computers to a globe-spanning network of connected computers suddenly allows us to share perfect copies of our work with a worldwide audience at essentially no cost.[1]

In the last three chapters we have moved from creating page images of part of a nineteenth-century book to having those images rekeyed and then producing some analytical files, such as lists. Along the way we have produced other files as well, and there are many more possibilities if work continued. As the project becomes more complex and the outputs more diverse, so we need to become more careful about managing all of this material effectively. The illustrative work we have done already on the Post Office directory has generated about a thousand files, representing different stages of the work, but a genuine digital history project could easily involve orders of magnitude more files and more complexity.

Our goal may well be to publish findings in some form, and to work rigorously through this process we will need to have everything properly managed. We do not want to be working on outdated versions of the files or to be unsure what happened to the list of professions from which we generated a particular chart. We especially do not want to produce a chart (which we are going to do in the next chapter) and then be unsure which version of our data it really comes from.

Digital history also tends to involve collaboration, openness and sharing. Because other historians may take different approaches to any data we share, or may want to enhance or manipulate it for different approaches and reasons, it is even more essential that the data they start their work with is clearly structured and well documented.

We begin by discussing data management and the importance of version control, both for collaboration and for solo research, and then move on to the importance of sharing data and the related questions of credit and licensing. We will devote a lot of time in this chapter to the Git program, because we think it can provide a solution to many of these questions. We hope to convince you that, for that reason, it is worth learning even a little bit of Git.

DATA MANAGEMENT

Digital history not only represents a shift in the way we undertake research, it fundamentally transforms how we share that research. There have never been more opportunities and means to share your research than there are today. Research output goes beyond paywalled journal articles and, indeed, need not include them at all. Throughout this book, you have been learning how to create and transform digital data. Let us consider some research outputs that can be generated from the Post Office project so far:

- Metadata
- Page images
- Machine-readable text in plain text format
- Machine-readable text in XML format

If we have done our work well, we have already produced many digital assets that are of interest not only to other academics but also to a much broader community, from family historians to the person researching the history of their house, from the local borough council to the researcher in Australia trying to track down the movements of a particular nineteenth-century individual. Managing the digital material we have produced is an added challenge – another thing to consider and learn how to do. But doing so effectively can mean that a text which was perhaps previously limited to a few academic libraries becomes accessible and discoverable in an entirely new way. It even becomes findable by people who were not specifically looking for it.

Our written research can also take a myriad of different shapes and be shared in many different ways. Some researchers have turned to commercial platforms such as Twitter, Facebook or Instagram to share their work in various formats. Other researchers blog on personal or institutional websites. Some researchers post videos about their work or discuss it on podcasts. Research can be shared at any stage of the process, and we can open up our work for comments and critique before submitting it for publication.

Even the most traditional of research outputs, the monograph and the peer-reviewed article, can be published under a variety of licences and with varying degrees of accessibility, the most open of which is open access. Open access, as defined by Peter Suber, one of its most vigorous supporters and articulate exponents, is 'digital, online, free of charge, and free of most copyright and licensing restrictions'.[2]

If we go into a project thinking about the outputs and thinking about how we can share those, we can bring a tremendous amount of value to the research community. In order to do this, however, we have to consider the future researchers who will benefit from our work from the very beginning of a project.

In previous chapters we have spoken of the need to be critical of all digital materials used in research: to ask how they were produced, to expect transparency, to look for clear documentation and metadata. In turn, as producers of digital materials we have a responsibility to ensure that future researchers will be able to interrogate our work in the same way. Is its production and processing transparent? Is the project well documented? Is the metadata intelligible?

There is someone else, who may be important to you, who will also benefit from this: your future self. By considering these questions throughout your work, you are ensuring that you can come back to this project six months or six years later. Our data is only useful if we can share it with others, and we must think of our future selves as strangers – strangers who will no longer understand this poorly documented decision or remember the meaning of this column labelled simply 'B'.

DATA MANAGEMENT AND VERSION CONTROL

In the excitement of beginning a new piece of research or a new project, it is incredibly tempting just to dive in and start doing things. If you have taken to heart our warnings that data cleaning is 80% of the work on the average digital project, you may be anxious to start on this straight away. It will stand you in better stead, however, if you take a moment to plan how you will manage your data and keep it safe. It will not delay you very long and you can then get your hands dirty. You will need to consider:

- metadata (how you describe your data, both internally and externally)
- version control (what to do if you mess things up)
- documentation (a narrative description of the project)
- preservation (how the data can be kept usable in coming years)

We are most familiar with metadata at the file level. The name itself is metadata, as are the file type, size and dates of creation and last update. A file such as an XML file may contain metadata in the header: we mentioned the TEI header at the end of the previous chapter, which has exactly this function. A photograph may come with standard metadata (known as EXIF) such as the type of camera and its settings, the geographic coordinates where the picture was taken and much more.[3] Reading a piece of code, especially in a programming language you do not know, can be a daunting prospect, but well-written code should contain comments which explain what it does and, in broad terms, how it does it.

You may want to create extra external metadata such as a manifest of your files. You might remember the `ls` command from Chapter 4: it has flags which can give more verbose information or recursively list all the files in all subfolders. As always with the command line, you can write your results to a file using > to redirect the output.

With images, you may want to add a description or tags which describe the subject of the picture in ways that you might want to find later, such as data, provenance or image type. We said in Chapter 2 that there are tools for managing images, such as Tropy for research photographs, which will help you manage your collection.

Your file structure is an important part of your metadata, but file structures can grow rather organically. This means many projects end up somewhat haphazardly organised, especially if multiple people are working on them. Give some thought to how your structure will work at the beginning. Try as far as possible to structure things around the natural workflow of the project. For example, where will the project's files be kept? Will files be copied? Will it be clear which files derive from which as they move through the workflow? All this can be made easier with good metadata.

As always, documenting these decisions immediately is useful. It may seem overkill to write down things like 'processed files are moved from folder X to folder Y', but you will almost certainly benefit from being explicit. Documenting as you go along will also make producing the final project documentation less painful.

VERSION CONTROL

Version control is essential. You will probably at some point have got confused about which version of a file is the latest, or where you got up to in a particular task, or you will have overwritten some work by accident. As projects become more complex, these problems can spiral.

At the absolute minimum you need two things: a coherent file-naming system and a plan for how to restore things if work is lost. Filenames like this are not recommended:

```
alice-extra-section-final-final.txt
bob-extra-section-really-final-txt
```

You can version files with numbers in a simple way, which is especially helpful if you are iterating over them with changes, for example:

```
post-office-v07.xml
post-office-v08.xml
```

Note that you probably want these to sort nicely, so we are using a leading zero. Otherwise, when you get to `post-office-v10.xml` it might sort above version 2; you might then not see it and create another version 10. If you are thinking of going above ninety-nine versions, we suggest your approach might need radically rethinking rather than just another zero. If each version is linked to a particular task or processing step in your documentation, identifying the origin of problems discovered later will be much easier.

This system is sustainable if you are working alone, but working collaboratively adds another level of complexity. If two people work on the same dataset then what happens to version numbers? If the same file is changed twice and the results need merging into one master version, who will do that and how hard will it be? This is why a good file-naming system is necessary but not adequate on its own.

Make a backup of anything you would rather not lose. That can be a local copy for quick and regular incremental backups, but really you should be planning for the catastrophe of your laptop breaking or being left on a bus, or your institutional file system becoming corrupted. The minimum here would be to email yourself a copy of the essential files. An external drive is a good option, but drives with their own power system are more robust than those without. If files are in a proprietary format, it is a good idea to export a backup to a different format so that you are never reliant on one piece of software.

Like anything in life, if it is important to you then you should schedule it (this is why people tend to schedule their wedding but not going to the gym). Set something in your calendar to remind you to back up on a suitable schedule, like weekly; do not rely on yourself to spontaneously remember to do it. You do not want the worst to happen when you have been *meaning* to back up for a few months but have not quite got round to it.

GIT

We believe that the gold standard for version control is the free program Git. We think it is so useful that we are going to spend quite a few pages describing the basics of how to use it.

Why are we so keen on Git and why do we want you to know about it? From our experience of working on digital history projects, we know that things go wrong. We have made many mistakes and we expect to make more in the future. Git enables us to rewind to the point where things went wrong and even to cherry-pick parts of later versions of files which we do not want to spend more time having to redo. Equally importantly, Git makes it easy to experiment, not simply in the knowledge that you can get back the file you just overwrote, but because its way of working actively facilitates experimentation.

Even if you do not ever plan to touch Git, it is so widely used that it is useful to know roughly how it works. A lot of digital humanities data is now made available as a public repository (a collection of files) where Git is used as the version-control system, as with the repository for this book. That means that some of the information about the project is kept in the logs which Git keeps, and you can easily access them if you know where to look.

If you become a bit more conversant with Git you could even restore someone else's project to an earlier stage. Suppose that, in reading through the Git logs, you see that an XML element was deleted at a certain point (in Git this means, as we shall see shortly, at the point of a particular commit) because it was considered irrelevant to the project's aims. Your research might be intensely interested in the deleted information and, happily, you can revert the files to restore it. This is possible because when you take a copy of a Git repository, you get the ability to replay that repository's entire history.

We can only give a quick run-through of Git's main features here, and for straightforward projects this may be all you need: a small amount of Git is enough to put your data under effective version control. Fortunately, much more information on Git can be found online. Chacon and Straub's online book *Pro Git* is clear and well organised.[4] If you get completely stuck then forums such as Stack Overflow (https://stackoverflow.com/) are a good place to discover that others have been puzzled by the same thing you are and have already been given advice.

Be aware that, in the scenario we are outlining here, Git does not provide you with a backup. If you do leave your laptop on the bus, the files are still lost to you.

At its most basic, Git keeps track of a set of files on your local machine. You specify what those files are and can commit them at any point where you have made changes. This allows you to recover the state of any file or files at any of the times when you committed it. For this reason, we suggest you commit frequently: it gives you more points for the recovery of your work.

There are graphical tools to help you use Git, but you can also use it on the command line, as we will do with this minimal example. Git is free and we will assume you have it installed. If you downloaded Git Bash for Windows, as advised in Chapter 4, you will have it already. For other operating systems, you will need to install it using your normal method of installing software.

Git works with files that are plain text. Git does not work well with formats like Microsoft Word's .docx. To start with you will probably want to use Git for research data rather than for narrative for publication. Having said that, this chapter was drafted in plain text, using Git for version control; we then converted from plain text to .docx using a free tool called Pandoc (https://pandoc.org/).

To start our Post Office project, we received one large file (all-b-streets.xml) from our keying company, which, if you have worked through chapters 4 and 5, you will remember well. We put this file into a folder initially called data. We wanted to put that folder, and any subfolders, under version control immediately, because we had just paid for the work to be done and did not want to lose it. We recommend that you copy the file into a new folder somewhere else on your file system and follow along.

First open the command line inside your new folder. To initiate Git here, we type:

```
git init
```

You should get some messages on the screen to tell you this has been done. This is great but at the moment *the folder is under version control with Git but the file is not*. You must explicitly tell Git to track files with git add, and we have not done that yet.

All Git commands start with git, so get used to typing it. In this case we type:

```
git add all-b-streets.xml
```

Remember when we were grepping all of the files in a folder using *.xml? The process for Git uses similar syntax:

```
git add *.xml
```

If you want to add everything of any file type whatsoever you can use a full point (.), like this:

```
git add .
```

You can keep adding files as they are created with successive use of git add.

The last step, and the one that seems confusing initially, is that we need to commit all the files that have been added. You might think that simply adding files means they can now be recovered, but by itself this is not sufficient. Files can only be recovered to the point at which they were committed, which we do after adding, like this:

```
git commit -m 'Post Office transcription as received from keyers'
```

In other words, Git adds the files you tell it to, and when you choose to carry out a commit all those added files are committed (and nothing else). In practice, you will soon find that this double step of adding and then committing gives you much more control over what you commit (if you add too much, you can also remove some files before you commit).

For example, if you create some temporary files, say from the output of a grep, you might not want them committed into the history of the project. If you do not explicitly add them, they will not be.

You will have seen above that we added a message with our commit using the -m flag. A commit message is mandatory and it is a great temptation when you have finished a chunk of work to write something like 'more work blah' in your message. Please resist this temptation. Commit messages are a very useful log of what was done on the project, so being meaningful and precise in your commit messages is advised. If you want to recover to a certain point before things went wrong, or to check what has changed, then messages to your future self or collaborators like 'more work' will be unhelpful. Another benefit is that if you are working on a long project, you do not need to scribble a note of where you got up to at the end of the day: just put it in the commit message and retrieve it the next day with `git log`.

At any time when you are working you can check which, if any, files have been changed since the last commit with:

```
git status
```

To see all the commits so far type:

```
git log
```

By default, the latest message is at the top. Here is the `git log` message for this chapter when it was first being drafted:

```
commit     a9aadf8a7fa1eba6bc52ec1233eee61d72ed9e52
(HEAD -> master, origin/master, origin/HEAD) Author:
Jonathan Blaney <jonathan.blaney@sas.ac.uk> Date:
Thu Mar 14 14:39:34 2019 +0000
Began writing Git section
```

Now you have your files under Git, how do you wind back the clock? The commonest thing you will do is to mess up a single file in some way. If this happened while editing our `all-b-streets.xml` file, we can recover it to the last commit with `checkout`:

```
git checkout all-b-streets.xml
```

Now the file will be back to the state it was in at our last commit. Any changes you made after that commit are lost irretrievably. This is why we say you should try to commit often. Every time you do a bit of work you would not like to lose, then commit it.

If you want to temporarily revert ('check out') the whole folder as it was at the last (or any other) commit, you need to specify the hash value for that commit. We have already seen one of these: it is the long number at the beginning of the log message above:

```
commit     a9aadf8a7fa1eba6bc52ec1233eee61d72ed9e52
(HEAD -> master, origin/master, origin/HEAD)
```

The hash value is a mathematical encoding of everything in the folder. It is always forty characters long, however much or little is in the folder. To the human eye, these values appear essentially arbitrary, so do not expect your sequential commits to have any hash values that display alphabetical or any other kind of ordering. To check out a whole commit, you must specify it by its hash value. Happily, you just need the first seven characters. So, to check out to the point where we wrote the message 'began writing Git section', the command is:

```
git checkout a9aadf8
```

In fact, tab completion means you do not even have to type the seven characters; key the first couple and the command line will offer you completions from the possible commits, of which there will be few, precisely because hash values appear to be random.

There is much more to learn with Git, but we would encourage you first to get comfortable with the workflow above. Then you can explore how to use a remote repository, using commands like `git push` and `git fetch`. With a remote repository comes the great advantage that you do now have a backup, because the work is mirrored remotely.

The most complicated step is working collaboratively in a shared repository, where you can use Git's excellent commands for *branching* (where experimental work can be done, away from the main branch) and *merging* back in.

As always, you do not want your first experience of checking out a file to be when you really, really need it to work. It is a good idea to practise: create a folder, put it under Git and mess around with a couple of dummy files. Commit, mess up, check out and repeat. To summarise, this is a sequence you will often go through:

- `git log` (see what the last commit message was)
- do some editing
- `git status` (see which files changed)
- `git add` (add the changed files that you want to keep)
- `git commit` (create a point to which you can revert later)

Even if you do not work with Git directly, you will probably come across other people's Git repositories. To work out what is in them, the conventional place for a summary is a file called README.md (the extension means it is a Markdown file: a text file with some light markup). If you do create a Git repository, you should create and use a README.md too. This file is part of a project's documentation, which leads us nicely on to the next section.

DOCUMENTATION

Documentation is the most neglected part of many digital humanities projects. Metadata and version control are unglamorous but generally recognised as important to start a project on a firm footing, so these form part of the set-up process. Documentation is normally left to the end of the project, for understandable reasons. Unfortunately, it is an iron law of these project life-cycles that the end is a frantic rush to get the data processed, the findings written up and maybe the website launched. Then everyone moves on to something else. Documentation gets squeezed out or inadequately done in this situation. It is only a few years later, when the people who worked on the project have forgotten parts of it, or are hard to contact, that the lack of good documentation really affects the usefulness of the project and its longevity.

We say this as guilty parties ourselves, not to castigate anyone else, but documentation deserves much better than this. One approach is to plan for an explicit period at the end of the project for documentation. This is a good idea, but if other elements of the work overrun, the documentation period is likely to become a buffer. Even a year later it can be hard to remember details from the beginning of the project that need to be documented (here we are thinking of any programme of research as a project: even small pieces of work can be frustrating to look back over if they are undocumented). So it is actually better to plan in documentation throughout the project: every time a decision is made or an observation about the work occurs, it can be added to a documentation file (which can be a bit rough and ready). At the very worst, the information is gathered; at best it can be organised and polished.

If you are working in a group, you will probably be taking meeting notes. Remember to treat these as project documentation in the fullest sense. If you treat them as a publicly available output from the beginning, it means you may not have to redact anything later.

If you are not using Git, we would encourage you to create a README file anyway. It does not have to be in Markdown, just to be in a format you are comfortable with, where you can quickly add notes about problems you have spotted, insights that have flashed into your brain, or choices you have made (and why). We repeat the same advice we gave above about Git commits: little and often. Add a few lines to your documentation every time something comes up and it will soon build up into a useful compendium of information about the project.

The documentation which can only be written at the end of the project would be the things that got away: projects have ambitions that are not realised and this is normal. Pointing the way towards future work is very helpful, whether it is suggestions of other datasets that could be used alongside yours, further data cleaning work that could be done, or ideas for coding. Do not be shy about publishing these. Incomplete projects are common. You never know, you might come back to the work later and find that someone has added to it, allowing you to take it further in turn. It should be obvious, as well, that this kind of openness is more likely to lead to future collaborations.

We have been treating documentation as a public output, meant for others to read and understand. That is an excellent approach and it is one we recommend you take even if you have no intention of ever publishing or sharing your project. We all have the illusion that what seems obvious to us now will remain so, but actually most people tend to forget details quickly. Write your documentation with this in mind and it will make you be much more explicit; you will take less for granted and be less cryptic, and so your documentation will be better. If you treat your future self as a stranger, you will not go far wrong.

DATA SHARING

Digital history projects tend to create a lot of data. This is true of any research, but digital data can be much more easily shared and reused than traditional paper files. As we have seen from Chapter 2, good data that has been cleaned and organised by people who understand it, accompanied by good documentation, is very valuable. We think it is good practice to make your data available to others once your project has finished, but there may also be, as we shall see, licensing reasons that mean you have to share your data. There will also be ethical considerations, particularly, as we discuss in Chapter 8, when recent history is the research topic, where the ease with which information can be accumulated and analysed may conflict with people's rights to privacy or wishes to be forgotten.

If you consider data as a research output from the inception of a project, it will help you to organise files in a way which might be helpful to others, not just to your immediate goals. For example, it can be easier and quicker to work with data which has had extraneous material cut from it. But the material which is superfluous to you might be the focus for someone else. By all means cut it out of your working files, but keep a copy from before the cuts were made and publish that too. Never assume that a particular piece of information could not be of interest to anyone.

We have already talked about the importance of documentation, and advising users on how to navigate the data is a good example of where future users can be helped. Good documentation will tell users things like 'For cleaned datasets, look here' or 'The plain text files in this folder are identical to the XML files in this folder, except in terms of markup'.

When researchers consider how to share their digital work, one option is usually the first thing that jumps to mind: create a website. Indeed, a website dedicated to a particular project can be a useful way to share the many outputs associated with that project. However, websites represent a significant investment of time and often money, and raise the question of sustainability. Even a project that has received extensive grant funding does not usually have funds that extend beyond the grant period in order to cover the continued costs of hosting and maintaining a website. This is a systemic problem in digital history, and leads to many excellent resources disappearing or being archived, making them hard to find and reconstruct.

A website requires regular maintenance. If you create one using a free and fairly intuitive platform such as WordPress, you will find that the platform (quite properly) produces a stream of updates, many of which are crucial to patch vulnerabilities that have been discovered. If you use plug-ins or other additional software which give you a particular type of functionality that you like or need, those too need updating. This need not be extremely onerous but it is an ongoing commitment for as long as the site is live.

Are you going to have an email address on your contact page or a webform that links to an email address? If so, then somebody needs to monitor that and perhaps even reply. Equally, a blog with comments often seems like a good idea, and often is a good idea, but blog comments may need to be moderated for years after you have stopped posting any content.

A sure-fire way to have users question the quality of your project is to host it on an out-of-date or only partially working website. Therefore, it is worth carefully considering alternatives before jumping in. If you want your digital project to have continued value to the research community, the sustainability of that work should not be an afterthought as you wrap up the project; it should be built into the project from the very beginning.

Your institution may commit to hosting a website for the medium or long term, but there are other options. If you have an affiliation, your institution probably has its own repository of research data and publication; these will archive, preserve and, hopefully, make accessible digital copies of your work. It may even be the case that your affiliation actually requires you to deposit some items there anyway. Such repositories should be professionally maintained and the data within them preserved and migrated to new software versions or formats as necessary. Data preservation is a technical skill; if you can get expert help by using an institutional repository then this is by far the best solution to a difficult problem. The ability to upload datasets is a standard feature of institutional repositories, but a member of staff would be able to advise you and maybe even carry out more complex tasks for you. A restriction you may find is that the per-item or per-collection metadata fields provided are restricted and do not cover everything you would like to include. Here you might consider adding some dedicated metadata files of your own as uploads. For ease of use and sustainability, institutional repositories are a reliable place to put your data, even if you also share that data in other ways as well.

There are also disciplinary repositories such as Humanities Commons, which is a non-profit, interdisciplinary platform; but commercial platforms are, as usual, the big players. We have mentioned GitHub several times, and that is where we are hosting the repository for this book, but there are others. Less technically focused sites which allow sharing are Dropbox and Google Docs. Basic use of these sites is normally free, but do, as always, check on the terms and conditions: who owns the data? Are you signing over control of anything? Does the platform have the right to reuse your data without asking you? Do you also have a copy elsewhere?

A final and rather basic approach is to put a dataset on a webpage as downloadable files or one zipped file of your data. This can be any webpage to which you are allowed to add files, so need not be part of a dedicated website. The file or files can be placed on the website's server and linked to from a single HTML page. A user clicking the links will be asked if they want to download the file. This keeps the process simple and within your control, but your data is likely to be found only by people who have first found the website.

When someone does find your dataset, how are they allowed to reuse it? This is your choice and you should specify it in a licence. You do not need to write a licence yourself, and it is probably not a good idea, because this work has already been done. For software there are licences such as the MIT License and GNU General Public License, but for humanities outputs we strongly recommend the Creative Commons (CC) licences. For a CC licence, there are multiple choices which give you fine control over how your work is reused. Table 6.1 outlines the main options.

You can mix and match CC licences: for example, CC-BY-NC would be a CC licence for reuse with attribution and provided it is for non-commercial purposes. CC0, meanwhile, is a very open licence and may be good for something like releasing photographs on sites such as Wikimedia Commons or Unsplash.[5] But for academic work, you clearly deserve credit and so CC-BY is often a good choice.

Given the kind of work done in digital history, and the benefits of others reusing your data, a no-derivatives licence, CC-ND, would be very unhelpfully restrictive and we recommend you avoid it. You might want to differentiate between a more open licence for data but something more restrictive for written outputs or other things you want to republish later, such as visualisations, video or sound recordings.

Table 6.1 Creative Commons licence types

Abbreviation	Description
CC0	the most permissive form of the licence: users can do what they like
CC-BY	the work can be used for any purpose, as long as attributed to its creator
CC-NC	the work can be used for any non-commercial purpose
CC-SA	the work can be used but resultant work cannot be published under a more restrictive licence
CC-ND	the work can be used but cannot be altered

It is quite common for researchers to publish their data only after they have published their own outputs, to ensure that they establish their priority. Institutional repositories should have this facility baked in (they have this because of the embargo periods common with journal publishing) and so you could put the data safely on a repository and then embargo it for a suitable period.

* * *

We began this chapter with an optimistic quotation from Peter Suber, strongly advocating the ability to share work 'at essentially no cost'. We think we have shown in this chapter that, much as we support data sharing, there are in fact considerable costs. We will talk more generally about the environmental costs of digital history in Chapter 8, but let us note here that having multiple copies of data does have an environmental impact: the digital is not, as is sometimes assumed, incorporeal. Throughout this chapter you will have noticed that there is considerable work involved in making data genuinely reusable. We think it is worth the effort, but the labour involved should not be underestimated.

NOTES

1 Suber, *Open Access*.
2 Suber, *Open Access*.

3 An entertaining exploration of metadata and its history is Gartner, *Metadata: shaping knowledge from antiquity to the semantic web*.
4 Chacon and Straub, *Pro Git*.
5 Wikimedia Commons, https://commons.wikimedia.org/wiki/Main_Page; Unsplash, https://unsplash.com/ (both accessed 10 July 2020).

» 7 «

VISUALISING YOUR DATA

> It is not how much information there is, but rather how effectively it is arranged.[1]

Up to this point we have been producing new digital data in primarily textual form, whether it is digitising an analogue text, as in Chapter 3, extracting information from the data, in chapters 4 and 5, or versioning and documenting it, as in Chapter 6. All of this was essentially internal project data, even though we suggested that it might be useful for others too. The present chapter turns to how you might visualise your data with the intention of sharing it with others. First, we will discuss the practice of visualisation and some of the doubts that have been raised about what is often regarded as 'best practice'. Next, we will look at how to derive numerical data from files in a form in which it can be visualised in charts and plots. Finally, we will come to producing maps and working with images generally. We will return to the Post Office data and produce charts and a map to illustrate what we mean. There are many other choices that we could have made with these, our own visualisations, and we make no claim that they could not be improved. Indeed, we encourage you to critique our efforts and consider what might be done better.

Although presentational visualisation will be our focus, there is not necessarily a sharp distinction between producing work for the consumption of others and developing your own ideas and gaining an overview of your data. Visualising your own data in a variety of ways can provide new insights or avenues for research, just as ideas often develop further in the course of being formally written up.

VISUALISATION AND HISTORICAL PRACTICE

Edward Tufte, the doyen of data visualisation, argues persuasively in favour of 'information-thick' rather than 'data-thin' public presentations of data. Otherwise, he argues, viewers will want to know what has been left out. At the same point in his book *Envisioning Information*, however, he also warns that showing such complexity is difficult and expensive, and gives as an example the skills involved in high-quality cartography.[2]

Visualising data, then, ought to be done thoughtfully and with a clear sense of what we are trying to achieve and how it integrates into the work as a whole. We may never quite reach the standards of high-class cartography, but we can avoid getting ourselves into situations where we need to generate some hasty graphs the day before submitting an article to a journal; and we can avoid some of the more common pitfalls in data visualisation.

As historians, we also need to remain attuned to what the data represents even as it is visualised. We are used to keeping in mind the ways in which the survival and the form of historical data reflects assumptions and values that led to its collection and its retention; we know that much has been lost and what remains may be uncertain or misleading. In *Seeing Like a State*, James C. Scott explores ways in which the desire of states for 'legibility' led to 'complex, illegible and local social practices' being forced by officials into 'a standard grid whereby it could be centrally recorded'.[3]

How are we to reconcile Tufte's insistence on legibility with Scott's on the complex and illegible? Johanna Drucker suggests, in a self-described polemical article, that we relabel data as 'capta', in etymological recognition that what we call data is not a given but what was taken, that knowledge is 'not simply given as a natural representation of a pre-existing fact'. Drucker is concerned that in visualisation specifically, 'we seem ready and eager to suspend critical judgement in a rush to visualization'.[4]

Drucker wants to include uncertainty in visualisation, and gives examples of how that might be done. D'Ignazio and Klein make a different critique of standard practices and advocate the inclusion of emotion – what they call to 'vicerealize' data. On this score they criticise Tufte's insistence that emotion should be excluded from visualisations as a 'false binary between emotion and reason', for which the logic is gendered.[5]

We think that most historians would agree with D'Ignazio and Klein. In studying the lives of others, empathy and compassion are surely prerequisites for any attempt at understanding. Perhaps in the past historians felt it appropriate to excise such feelings from their published texts, but few today would follow Conrad and Meyer's practice of blank neutrality in describing US slavery in terms of economic units that we noted in Chapter 1.

We think that Ducker's admonition is valuable. Visualisation is not a separate arena for the historian. We should try to make our visualisations convey what we wish to show throughout our work, and part of that may indeed be uncertainty, compassion and at least something of the lived reality behind the historical enquiry.

To return to the distinction made above, a consideration here is who the visualisation is intended for. The debate between Tufte and critics such as D'Ignazio, Klein and Drucker presupposes presentational visualisation of results already known to the researchers. Drucker's consideration of ways to convey uncertainty envisages researchers who already know of that uncertainty and audiences who do not.

If you are working with a lot of data, it can be very useful to produce lots of quick visualisations for you and any collaborators to look through and compare side by side. These need not meet the canonical standards for clarity or information thickness; they are a finding aid to patterns in the data. If you are generating hundreds of plots or charts then your natural human aptitude for pattern recognition will mean that interesting or rogue results will leap out of the data. To do this you need a tool that is fast, and we would recommend gnuplot, which is free and cross-platform, and works from the command line; because it has been around for a long time, it also works in concert with lots of other software.[6] Gnuplot is much used by scientists but it is effective for anyone with lots of data to handle; it can tile numerous plots or charts in a gallery for quick viewing. You can do the same thing with programming languages such as R and Python if you prefer. Nathan Yau's *Visualize This* contains some very clear examples using R which require no prior knowledge of programming.[7]

A subsidiary benefit to quickly generating visualisations like this is that, as Yau points out, outliers or unexpected patterns may simply indicate errors, so visualisation can be part of data cleaning.[8] In this way, messiness becomes almost the point of the exercise and, for historians, takes us back to what we knew all along: that data is contingent, partial and rarely as tractable as a clean and polished published visualisation might suggest.

VISUALISING NUMERICAL DATA

We will approach this task in two phases. First, we will extract some numerical data from the Post Office material directly into a format in which a visualisation program can make use of it. Second, we will investigate ways in which this data can be plotted and choose the methods which seem most appropriate to us. This extracted data is available in our repository and we very much hope that you will experiment with it for yourself.

What we are concentrating on here is the manipulation of the data itself: extracting and manipulating numbers from data sources. The statistical analysis of that resulting data and what evidential weight it can bear is a more complex question. On this latter process we can say very little: statistical claims about historical data is not an area of digital history per se but a specialist area with many subtleties. Trained statisticians themselves often, in good conscience, disagree with each other about the significance and meaning of results.[9] David Spiegelhalter, who specialises in communicating statistics to the public, warns that:

> Far from freeing us from the need for statistical skills, bigger data and the rise in the number and complexity of scientific studies makes it even more difficult to draw appropriate conclusions. More data means that we need to be even more aware of what the evidence is actually worth.[10]

This is a counsel of caution, not of despair. Unless you have strong statistical experience, we advise that you concentrate upon what Spiegelhalter calls forensic statistics: 'There is no mathematics, no theory, just a search for patterns that might lead to more interesting questions.'[11]

If your research depends upon statistical analysis of any complexity, we would advise you to check with an expert before publishing conclusions drawn from it. This is an area where the untrained, and even the trained, can go astray.[12]

Better news is that many of the techniques covered in the chapters on working with text will work just as well with numbers found in running text or in tables. As has been a theme of this book, much of the work again lies in data cleaning and processing. Yet again, regex will be a key tool here, not just in extracting the numbers you are interested in but also in formatting them into a usable structure for your next steps.

What you use now depends on your goals and their complexity. A spreadsheet program such as Microsoft Excel can do many number-crunching tasks. But if you are doing anything very complex you may need to learn and use a dedicated program. Two examples of free software much used in digital humanities are the statistics program R and the libraries which come with the general programming language Python (such as the library NumPy). We must also make mention of the commercial software SPSS, which is used in the social sciences. Because it is widely used in universities, if you have a university affiliation you may have both access to SPSS and training in using it.

There are a couple of caveats to using spreadsheet programs (for which we will use 'Excel' as shorthand). Excel does not automatically have field controls to prevent you from adding the wrong kind of values or data that becomes nonsensical in the wrong context. By contrast, when you create a database you must specify what type of data can go in each field, and this in itself should stop a user from adding text to an integer or date field. You can set field controls in Excel, but most people do not and, crucially, if you open data in Excel you cannot set the types in advance; this can irrevocably destroy the original values. Excel tries to helpfully detect the type, but can easily get it wrong. For example, long numbers (123456789) might be changed to scientific notation and take a form like 1.23E+08, or a numeric range like 1–20 becomes the date '20 January'. In a large spreadsheet you may never know that these changes have been made.

Because Excel is in widespread use, there are many stories of data gone bad associated with it. It was designed for businesses to use and works well for financial data. The fault was probably not with Excel but with the choice to use it.[13] Excel is a reasonable choice for simple calculations, but we agree with the mathematics communicator Matt Parker that, 'doing any kind of important work in a spreadsheet is not a good idea'.[14]

Excel can open CSV and TSV files. It will repeatedly offer to save the file in its own format, .xlsx, but this can be ignored. We recommend using TSV for your own data before opening it in Excel. This is because your data is unlikely to have tabs in it: the separator should ideally be something which is not used for anything else in the file. Commas in historical texts are, of course, highly likely to be used as ordinary commas. As you will have seen, the Post Office listings may contain multiple commas per line.

If we want to do some calculations in Excel on the data we have been working on, how might you go about it? We can use `grep` to extract some text from a collection of XML files, add tabs using regex and paste the result into an Excel spreadsheet as TSV. A tab character can be substituted in regex by using \t in the replacement field.

First, we will try something we did in Chapter 5: to extract the professions from our street listings. This time, however, we will sort the most frequent occupations to the top of the list:

```
grep -Eoh ",[^,]+</addr>" *.xml | sort | uniq -c |
sort -nr
```

Do you remember how this works? Do not worry if not, but we would really encourage you try this out. Try breaking the command down from left to right and then building it back up, running it bit by bit. We have put a full explanation in a text box if you need to check your understanding.

> **Extracting the professions**
>
> First, as a rough proxy for professions, we want to find everything after the final comma in a listing. This calls for a regex, introduced by grep -E. We only want the results, not the whole line, so that requires grep -o. Finally, we will add an -h flag to grep to suppress the filenames, otherwise we will not be able to group professions together because each line's filename will make it unique:
>
> ```
> grep -Eoh
> ```
>
> The regex is , [^,]+</addr> – this looks for a comma, a space, then anything other than a comma, followed by </addr>. We do it this way as a means of selecting the final comma in the line. There might also be useful professions information before the final comma; to check that, we can use a more inclusive regex: ,.+</addr>. Try them both out and see the differences. So, now we have a listing of every result in all the files, one per line, with this command:
>
> ```
> grep -Eoh ",[^,]+</addr>" *.xml
> ```
>
> We want a count of unique professions strings now, but first we have to sort (the uniq command requires text that is already sorted), then we can count unique examples:

VISUALISING YOUR DATA   129

```
grep -Eoh ",[^,]+</addr>" *.xml | sort | uniq -c
```

Finally, we want to sort again. Now we have numbers, we want to sort on the numbers with sort -n. With no other flags, this sorts 1, 2, 3, and so on, but we are most interested in the high numbers, so we will reverse the numerical sort with sort -nr. Here is the whole thing:

```
grep -Eoh ",[^,]+</addr>" *.xml | sort | uniq -c |
sort -nr
```

The first lines of your results should look roughly like this:

```
199 , baker</addr>
163 , grocer</addr>
152 , tailor</addr>
148 , solicitor</addr>
128 , bootmaker</addr>
127 , greengrocer</addr>
124 , beer retailer</addr>
118 , butcher</addr>
116 , chandler's shop</addr>
112 , sec</addr>
109 , coffee rooms</addr>
101 , tobacconist</addr>
```

First, we will write these results to a file with a .tsv extension: use the up arrow to go back through your command history to the long command we just entered. Then add > professions.tsv onto the end, so the full command is now:

```
grep -Eoh ",[^,]+</addr>" *.xml | sort | uniq -c |
sort -nr > professions.tsv
```

This will create a new TSV file, so open professions.tsv in your text editor. You will need to manipulate the text so that all the lines are formatted like this, where there is a tab between the number and the profession:

```
199 baker
163 grocer
152 tailor
```

These are two regexes and one literal find and replace. Try to do it yourself first before looking at our method in the endnote![15]

The text is now ready for Excel or equivalent. The easiest way to open it is to drag the TSV file to the Excel icon (or the window of the program, if it is already open). The other option is to select Excel on your system as the program with which to open TSV files.

Do not think of this as a one-way street: once the data is in Excel you can still manipulate it as text, either by opening your TSV or CSV files in a text editor, or on the command line. The facility to use different tools is a good example of why we prefer the plain text format wherever possible. If you just want to manipulate part of the data, it is often easier to paste just a single column or a couple of columns into a text editor, use regex to make any changes and then paste back into Excel. The reason for this is that if you have many columns to operate on, confining a regex to one column becomes a complicated business and one which is easy to get wrong. In general, regex is not the right tool for working with the structure of a document, which is what you are doing if you target changes to one column in a spreadsheet.

Let us leave aside concerns about the accuracy of the data collected by the agents for the Post Office directory (which we know to be full of errors because of the sample checking of the data done by Atkins[16]) and think about two aspects of the digital use of the data. The first is that transcription, by whatever method, is not an error-free process. We need not only to keep this in mind when considering the validity of our results but also to be open about the degree of accuracy in any outputs from the research, such as publication. The second aspect is that the numbers we can derive from the data are often derived from some form of counting. Digital tools give us fast and convenient ways of counting things, but we have to be careful that what is being counted is what we think is being counted.

To give a simple example, if someone wanted to count the number of women mentioned in the street directory the old-fashioned way, with a print copy of the book and a pencil and paper, they could choose some sample streets and meticulously read down the entries looking for female titles. They would probably be keenly aware of two things: that their sample could be skewed and not representative, and that they may miscount through human error. This would be a laborious process and the difficulty of properly sampling streets might then mean it is a waste of time.

The temptation is to think that machines do not tire or make mistakes and that it would thus be possible to run a count of female titles in a digitised street directory and get an accurate answer instantly. But what do we mean by female titles? A person reading entry by entry would intuitively recognise, say, 'Marchioness' or 'Signora' as female titles, but a search will only include 'Marchioness' and 'Signora' if explicitly told to.

There are many exotic ways to visualise the information we have just produced. If you are already experienced in using them, you do not need our advice. Here we will concentrate on the basic of producing good scatterplots and bar charts, with a mention of other possibilities such as histograms and sparklines. If you are not so experienced, we advise that you master these fundamentals before moving on to more obscure techniques.

A visualisation should be understandable in its own terms, and not require explanation in running text (captions, legends and so on are part of the visualisation). This means that the axes of charts should be labelled and, if numeric, should start at zero unless you have a strong reason not to.[17] It is normally good practice to use tickmarks (little ruler-like gradations along the axes which provide a readable scale or orientation for the eye), and do not forget to include an informative title.

You should try to avoid what Tufte has labelled 'chartjunk' – elements which are an unnecessary distraction from the information the reader needs to access. For example, Tufte says that dark gridlines are chartjunk and he suggests you try to lighten them or eliminate them altogether.[18] The focus should always be on the information, which can be complex and should not be simplified. As we argued at the beginning of the chapter, the danger of misleadingly simplified or cleaned information is perhaps more acute for the types of information that historians tend to want to visualise. This is the challenge.

It may seem unadventurous, but for comparing static figures against each other, a bar chart may the best option when the values are too numerous to be easily compared in a table. What is that tipping point between table and chart? This varies, because some people simply prefer visual displays over textual descriptions, or vice versa; but once you get into double figures, we suggest that you should start thinking about a chart rather than a table. The horizontal lines of a bar chart are what makes small-scale differences visible, so when values are close you should prefer a chart to a plot or, especially, a pie chart.

Pie charts showing a total quantity, like a national budget, may make an ideological assertion: whether a budget is a fixed quantity could be a matter of opinion. A pie chart gives the impression that there is a fixed limit to a particular quantity or resource: a bigger piece of pie for one member of the family, the narrative seems to go, means less for someone else. Hudson and Ishizu argue that pie charts are 'useful where there are relatively few variables which make up proportions of the whole'.[19]

This may ultimately be a matter of taste, but we believe that pie charts should be used sparingly, because it is very hard to compare quantities across the pie. We are not very practised at visualising what 10% of a circle, expressed as 36 degrees in a pie chart, looks like. Similar quantities like 32 and 35 degrees will look very similar in wedge form: if you label the wedges with the quantities you may ask why these figures could not go into a table instead. A pie with many slices, one for each figure, is hard to label easily such that the reader can see what each slice represents. It is perhaps this difficulty which leads to the use of the exploded pie chart, the separation of one or more segments from the whole, which makes it even harder to compare the sizes of slices. A final problem with pie charts is that they are reliant on colour and good colour choices (see our warnings about colour below). We are not saying there are no good pie charts in existence; but if you feel like creating a pie chart, think carefully about how to make it an effective one.[20]

A time series is good candidate for a scatterplot, especially when several different quantities are changing in relation to each other or there are sudden spikes in values. If we had the data from many decades of Post Offices directories, we could display the rise and fall of different, related professions. For example, we might chart the number of blacksmiths and car mechanics in the data over the period 1850 to 1950. We would expect the former to fall and the latter to rise, of course, but the point at which the line showing mechanic numbers crosses the descending line of blacksmiths might be surprisingly late, or early.[21]

Why not use a bar chart for this? Well, let us think about the data we are visualising. As we have mentioned several times, the Post Office data is not reliable: it does not give us the exact numbers of members of a profession in London in any one year. Because this data is indicative, a scatterplot which shows a trend over time is much more appropriate. A bar chart might encourage the reader to think of the figures as more precise than they are, and to attribute meaning to slight differences in values from year to year: this is misleading.

A histogram is similar to a bar chart but it has only one variable. So if you wanted a snapshot of just the blacksmith profession over the decades covered by the Post Office directory for a particular year, this would be a histogram (the variable is the number of blacksmiths). Histograms are particularly suited to statistical data because, for example, you can readily see if what they show conforms to a known statistical pattern like a bell curve. In our blacksmiths example, we would expect at some point to see their numbers steadily falling and any deviation from the trend would be worth investigating.

Finally, 'sparklines' (or 'line charts') are a useful method of compressing data to show an overall trend.[22] They look something like a freehand squiggle and are meant for a quick comparison of multiple trends, which can be placed in close proximity. If we had calculated the mortality rates for different streets in our London data over some decades, we could produce sparklines for each street. We would perhaps be expecting an upward squiggle across most streets, but any departure from whatever the trend is, such as a sudden rise or fall would be something to investigate in the history of that street. Sparklines, then, can be used for both of the categories of visualisation we have discussed: they can be a research practice and, because your audience may be equally interested in these trends, an output.

For the first of our two attempts at visualising the Post Office data we have been working with, we decided to look at the professions information we extracted using `grep`. We covered this in Chapter 5 and recapitulated it above, when discussing how to paste it into Excel.

As you will see, we ended up thinking that a fairly conventional stacked bar chart was the best choice for our visualisation. Our thought process recapitulated many themes we have already touched on throughout the book: inherent biases in the data, errors in the data, noise in our methods of extracting the information, our own choices in how we clean and present the data.

Finally, we can come to the question of what this means. We said in Chapter 3 that, in our experience, data cleaning takes up a large amount of time in digital history projects. This was the case with the professions data we used for the following visualisations. The majority of our time was spent cleaning up what we initially produced using `grep`. Our work on this is in the `data` folder of the repository, in the folder `professions-data`. The file's `*professions.csv` is the result of the `greps` we used to extract professions in Chapter 5. If you open the file, you will immediately see the noise we get along with the useful data, because the file is sorted with the upper-case strings at the top (normally professions in the directory are in lower case).

The entirely extraneous data in the file includes things like 'Col. Vickers' and 'F.R.M.S'. The initial process was simply to look through the list and to manually delete things like this from the upper part. While doing so, we began to see other types of problems, such as:

- Professions preceded by extraneous information such as company names
- Upper-case variants of professions, for example 'Butcher'
- Plural variants of professions, for example 'merchants'
- Abbreviation variants, for example 'mfrs' and 'mfs'
- Possible variants of professions, for example 'carpenter' and 'cabinet maker'
- Institutional names which might imply a profession, like 'coffee house'

At this point we had to make a number of decisions, all of which are contestable. We decided to delete things like 'coffee house' and 'lodging house' because we could not be sure of the role of the person listed – whether they were an owner, a manager or something else. We merged some professions; for example, we decided that 'pork butcher' could simply become 'butcher' for this exercise. We left others separate: we thought that 'carpenter' and 'cabinet maker' were sufficiently different and should not be merged. None of these decisions were taken without self-doubt.

Much of this was painstaking work, with not many obvious shortcuts that we could see. The advantage is that it forced us to look at and think about our results closely prior to visualising them. If we had acquired a perfectly clean dataset of professions from elsewhere, we may not have been quite so attentive.

Once the data had been cleaned, we then had to decide what was worth visualisation. The top ten male professions were solicitor, baker, boot maker, grocer, tailor, chandler, butcher, beer retailer and greengrocer. We could see nothing worth visualising here. What would be gained that could not be shown in a table? The presence of 'solicitor' at the top of the list cast doubt on our original idea of comparing male and female counts for the top male professions: women were not allowed to become solicitors until 1919, after the passing of the Sex Disqualification (Removal) Act.[23]

Instead, we decided to visualise the top ten female professions and look at how many men had that same profession listed. Our stacked bar chart of those professions can be seen in Figure 7.1. The software we used was Vega, an open-source web application for data visualisation.[24]

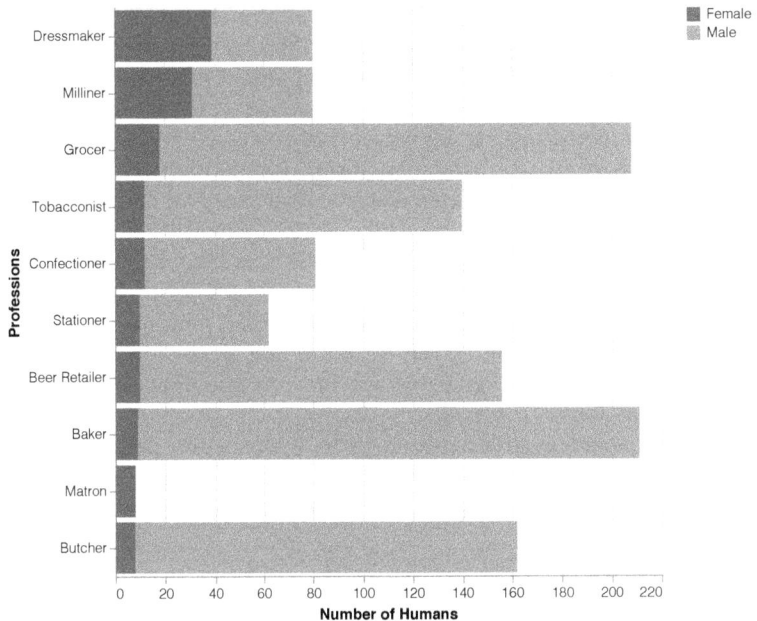

Figure 7.1 Top ten female professions

This visualisation immediately showed us something we had not noticed from looking at the data up to that point, which is that even these are professions dominated by men. This is the case not just for professions like butcher, which we might expect, but for dressmaker and milliner. Some of these look like data problems to be further investigated. As we said, visualisation can be an effective way of showing errors in your process.

To check on why there are so many milliners and dressmakers listed as men we could grep the original streets data (either the XML or the plain text) to look at some results. Doing this immediately showed us a significant problem in our procedure. In Chapter 5 we said that we would use 'Mrs' and 'Miss' as an approximation for identifying women. We thought that, in aggregate, other female titles would be rare enough to be unimportant for generating figures. A grep for milliner or dressmaker shows that many women in these professions have the title Madame. A subsequent grep for 'Madame' shows that dressmaker and milliner account for nearly all of the occurrences of this title in the data. Our decision to ignore variant titles like this may have been reasonable for most purposes, but for this particular category of female professions it was not. We have not done this here, but we can adjust the visualisation to account for this very quickly.

Since we have an easy division into professions of married and unmarried women, we then produced a stacked bar chart for the top female professions to show this division (Figure 7.2). You will notice that this is not the same list we used before. Rather than take the top ten professions for all women, we took the top ten professions for married and unmarried women. Because there are some overlaps, with some professions being in the top ten for both, that gives us fifteen professions. Our reason for doing this was that the visualisation now gives equal weight to both categories.

The immediately striking thing to us is that some professions are mostly represented by unmarried women, like grocer and tobacconist, while others, like stationer and staymaker, are mostly represented by married women.

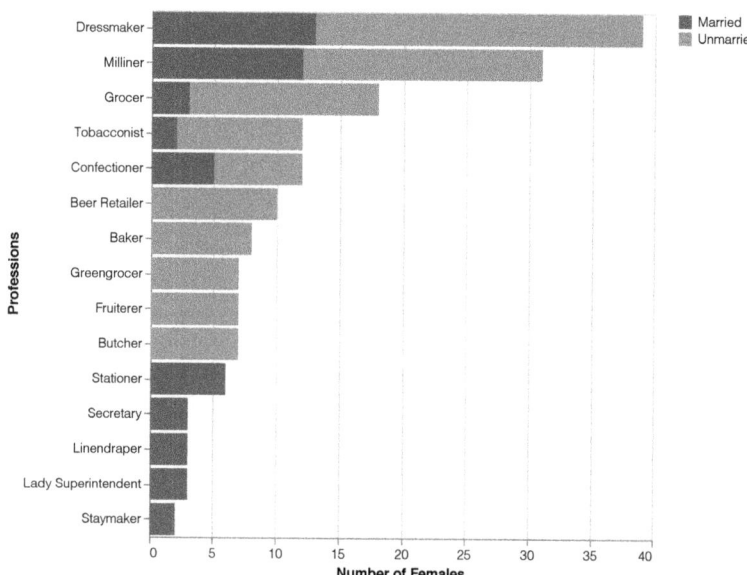

Figure 7.2 Top female married and unmarried professions

This brings us to the question of what the visualisation means. The numbers here are so low that it is hard to be sure that they are meaningful. Indeed, the professions with higher numbers seem to show a more even distribution than the lower counts.

This cannot be a finished visualisation for publication, not least because we are not subject experts. None of us are historians of nineteenth-century London. If we were though, and if we had all the streets rekeyed, these visualisations might just lead us to new avenues of research.

You will have noticed that our stacked bar charts are in greyscale. For this book we cannot use any colour images, and that is a common condition of print publication. Part of the difficulty of data visualisation for historians comes from their common methods of publication: print books and journals. Traditionally, except in rare instances, journals have not allowed colour illustration. If our stacked bar charts contained many categories, rather than just two, they would become hard to read in greyscale. For an online-only publication, of course, colour will not be a problem; for journals and articles published both online and in print it is likely that the digital version can be colour and the print black and white, but you would need to check with your publisher. There seems to be a trend towards more journals allowing colour, but be sure it can be used before you even plan your visualisations.

If you can use colour, your first concern is to make your work equally usable by people with colour vision deficiency. There are a number of types of colour vision deficiency but you can cater to all but the most rare by taking a couple of precautions.[25] Try not to make understanding the visualisation dependent on colour discrimination alone; use different intensities of colour next to each other, such as a dull colour paired with a vibrant one. If you know someone with colour vision deficiency, ask them to check your work but do not assume they are representative.

You may have noticed that we are sceptical about pie charts. Use of colour is another problem in producing them: colourful pie charts are engaging, but what do the colours mean? Do they simply differentiate slices? If so, brighter colours will pop out more and give undue prominence to certain slices. As many optical illusions show, our brains construct relative colours and shapes rather than taking everything in at once.[26] This is something to be borne in mind in all colour visualisation.

It is sensible to use colours that are naturally associated with something: a chart of gold and silver exports could intuitively use gold and silver. What you must avoid is using colours stereotypically associated with gender, ethnicity, sexuality or religion. With care, an image of the object can be used in a plot: Tufte has a particularly fine example of this in a plot of the size of animals, for which he has redrawn the original plot by replacing dots with outline drawings of each animal.[27]

MAPS

Maps have always been of great interest to the military, for both offensive and defensive operations. The first comprehensive mapping of Great Britain was done by the Ordnance Survey in the nineteenth century and, as its name suggests, was a military project. Nowadays the Global Position System, better known as GPS, used in most phones, is run and paid for the by the US military. However, modern maps do not match the nineteenth-century Ordnance Survey ones exactly, and older maps will vary far more.

GPS uses satellites to triangulate a position on the earth's surface, which is why it is better at detecting position in terms of the points of the compass rather than how high up something might be; for example, two floors of the same building might have the same coordinates. GPS is just one example of the technological aids that were not available to earlier editions of the Ordnance Survey, but there is a further reason why historical maps do not match modern satellite mapping. The earth's surface is three dimensional but maps are generally two dimensional, and the translation of one into the other, known as 'geodesy', can be done in different ways. You are probably familiar with the way in which different projections of the globe, such as Mercator and Gall–Peters, can make our two-dimensional world look very different (essentially, they all make compromises in different ways) but the same is true at much smaller scales too.

Working with maps is a natural thing for historians to do. There are good, free tools available to help them do so but, broadly speaking, the older the source of the maps the more work there is in getting those tools to use the digitised versions. For example, we saw above that 'baker' was a very common occupation description in our Post Office data. We could use a nineteenth-century map of London to plot all of the bakers listed in the directory to test the hypothesis that bakers will be very dispersed throughout a city (because bread is a good which spoils very quickly, so people want to buy it locally); we could make a comparison with tailors (fifth on our list) whose product is not perishable and so might be expected instead to show the clumping effect known as 'agglomeration'.[28] In fact London still has two streets particularly known for tailoring – Savile Row and Jermyn Street (other London tailors are available) – but not, as far as we know, for bakers: Bread Street, in the City of London, was the result of medieval fiat rather than agglomeration.[29]

To depict all of this you may not need any tools other than Adobe Illustrator or Inkscape, a scan of an appropriate map and some patience. However, if you want to add features to a map automatically, rather than manually adding them, you will need to use modern maps with some kind of Geographic Information System (GIS) interface, which manages that geographical data for you. Again, it may not matter to you that there are slight differences in where those features appear. Say, for example, you want to map plague sites in Wales in the seventeenth century; if a modern Welsh city centre is half a mile from its seventeenth-century equivalent, this does not greatly matter because the map's scale renders the difference negligible.

A reason not to use Google Maps or OpenStreetMap for the nineteenth-century bakers and tailors is that London streets have changed names and shapes since then; some have disappeared and more have been created. In the aggregate you might decide that this is acceptable in return for the ease of use modern maps offer. This is a trade-off that will be largely dictated by the goal of visualisation. Whatever you decide, we would suggest that Google Maps remains a good way to start experimenting with maps, because the interface is so easy to use. You can upload a spreadsheet with names and coordinates and Google Maps will add pins for you. To test a map, this is a good first approach; if you later decide Google Maps does not meet your needs, you can always go on to more powerful software. Although OpenStreetMap is an admirable project, we cannot recommend it for beginning mapping of this kind, because the various interfaces and tools available are both powerful and difficult to learn.

How can you get hold of the necessary coordinates? There are many solutions, from going to the location and using your phone or other GPS-enabled device, to using an online map or service that offers coordinates (such as GeoNames or OpenStreetMap). Often an easy solution is to leverage the work of others and look at what geographical information Wikipedia offers. For example, for the entry on Savile Row, Wikipedia offers us a download of the Keyhole Markup Language (KML) file for the street. KML is a format designed for representing geographical coordinates and happens to be the format used by Google Maps.[30]

We have mentioned GIS already, and it is a term much used in historical mapping. It refers to any system that interfaces a set of knowledge about the world (the location of Hong Kong or the River Danube, for example) with a mapping display system. Google Maps and Google Earth, then, are a form of GIS. The standard mapping software used in the humanities and social sciences was ArcGIS, a powerful and fairly expensive tool; if you have access to this via an institutional licence, we recommend using it, as well as taking the training that should be available institutionally too.[31] However, there is an excellent free competitor, QGIS, which may well meet all of your needs.[32] These tools give you the capability to carry out sophisticated mapping and geographical analysis, and to translate between the different coordinate systems that are in use.

A single point is described by a coordinate system, such as latitude and longitude, but to define an area in digital mapping requires a shapefile. This is a set of points which defines a polygon within a GIS. So there might be a shapefile for the city of Leicester or the county of Cumbria. Unfortunately, but interestingly for historians, the boundaries of cities and counties change over time; counties, cities, towns and villages appear and disappear; rivers change their course. As you can imagine, acquiring shapefiles for a modern entity is much easier than for its medieval equivalent.

Geocoding is the process of connecting an object with its location in the real world on a map. If you take a photograph with a modern camera, including the one in a smartphone, geographical information is automatically added to the metadata linked to the photo (unless this feature is turned off or your device settings remove the location metadata when sharing the photo). If coordinates are attached to your image, this would then allow you to locate your photo of, say, Brewer Street, London, on a map; but not just that: it would potentially allow you to group your images by location, to search for the most northerly photo you have taken, to associate the image with ones produced by others at the same location, or any other geographical use you can think of. You can also do this manually by adding the information yourself, such as in a caption, or on a map interface which allows you to drag an image to the location. This is not confined to photographs: we could imagine, say, working with the paintings and drawings of the Camden Town Group artists, associated with North London, and placing them on an appropriate map.

Georectification is the alteration of an image so that it 'fits' with a modern coordinate system within a GIS. This is frequently applied to older maps (for example, so that features and changes over time can more easily be overlaid and compared with the modern map). As you will imagine, the older the map the more rectification there will need to be: our map of late nineteenth-century London probably fits the modern coordinates quite well (other changes to the built environment aside), but a seventeenth-century map of London would be a different matter. Normally, the older image is stretched and warped to fit the new reality, but there are additional techniques to try to correct for this. If this sounds complicated, then it is: of the mapping approaches we have discussed, this is the most difficult and the one where you might want to seek advice from more experienced practitioners before diving in.

These obstacles do not preclude a simple approach to mapping, which we will adopt with our Post Office data. We can map a street and its cross streets by tracing an image or enhancing an existing map. (We do not believe this infringes copyright, but you should always check for yourself.) However, again, be aware that modern maps may not have the same street configuration as 1878.

Tracing maps may sound like a 1950s geography lesson, but some outstanding digital history projects use exactly this method. For example, the researchers behind the MAGIS Brugge project are redrawing a sixteenth-century map of Bruges,[33] and estimate that they have already spent longer tracing and enhancing the map than cartographer Marcus Gerards took to create the original. In much simplified form, we went through the following process.

We obtained from a colleague a digital copy of a map from 1897, on which he had already done quite a lot of processing and cleaning. We decided that this was close enough to our date for the map to be usable.

We started with a discussion about what we wanted to achieve generally: to combine the individual buildings along the postman's walk onto the map image and then to annotate some aspects of the data, as far as we could without overcrowding the map. After brainstorming how to visualise one specific street, Beaufort Street, we came up with some ideas about how to draw the buildings onto the map and colourise the buildings according to either gender or occupation type. One of the requirements was that the visualisation should be printed in greyscale, so all graphic design steps needed to ensure that the visualisation would be comprehensible in both colour and greyscale.

We then began by gathering various digital files ('assets' in graphic design terminology) and putting these into a directory. This included the map images themselves, the page scans of the Post Office directory and the XML data.

The graphic design application we used is fairly new and is called Affinity Designer. We decided to use this because it is reasonably priced, not a cloud-based subscription and combines image editing features for both 'raster' and 'vector' graphics into a single application. Raster graphics are based on pixels and so have a specific resolution, as with a digital photograph (as you zoom into a raster graphic it will at some point become pixellated); vector graphics are generated from mathematical equations (you can keep zooming in because the equation is recalculated by the program and never become pixellated).

We also wanted to learn to use some of the features of this new application, so a new Affinity Designer document was created and the digital assets placed into layers in the document. As we began to crop each cross street and align it over the top of the map, we realised the orientation of the map needed to be adjusted. To ensure we used the correct compass north, we found Beaufort Street on the Apple Maps application, took a screenshot of the compass, imported the image onto our old map and rotated all the assets into position, for the first version (Figure 7.3).

We then proceeded to draw building outlines along each of the street blocks, and cropped, overlaid and scaled the property numbers from the Post Office directory text, to help get a sense of the size of each building (Figure 7.4). This informed the drawing of the building or terrace walls. We originally used red lines to make them stand out more, but converted the lines to black later. The background map included more of the surrounding streets, so we feathered and blurred these out towards the edges to maintain the viewer's focus on Beaufort Street.

Now that the building artwork had been generated to scale, we decided which feature to use and which colour code would work for each of the buildings. We decided to colour-code for gender, using pink for male and blue for female.

The vector shapes of the buildings were duplicated into a second layer and rasterised (turned into pixels), then each block could be filled with the appropriate colour, according to the title of the occupant (or if a title was not present in the listing, we made a judgement based on the person's name, in the knowledge that the text identifies females explicitly and males implicitly). There was one address which listed a male and female, and for this we simply pained both colours into the space. Once the colours had been filled, to emphasise these as 'atop' the map, a drop

Beaufort st, *Chelsea.***(S.W.)**
Map G 13.

WEST SIDE.
1 Long Miss
3 Ellis Misses, ladies' school
7 Bell Geo. Graham, land surveyor
9 Winsland Mrs
11 Palmer Miss
13 Thompson Miss
15 Smith Mrs
17 Innous Thomas Pippet
19 Pecek Mrs
21 Saunders Mrs
25 Delarue Theodore
27 Royle Joseph
31 Robert Charles Pierre
33 Dike Mrs
37 Marlow Mrs
39 Wilson Thos. Harrington, artist
41 Reid Andrew, artist
43 Hughes Mrs
45 Collins William
47 Little William, travelling draper
49 King Alfred
51 Goldie Bruce
53 Sweeney Hugh Willoughby
    Wright Mrs.Catherine,lace cleaner
63 Williams Charles, cowkeeper
    .... *here is King's road* ....
67 Spaull George, marine store dealr
69 Taylor William, fishmonger
71, 73 & 75 Somes Major, unre-
    deemed pledge stores
77 Palmer John, grocer
79 Chandler George, dairyman
81 Green Thomas, butcher
83 Brooks John, bootmaker
    Holmes George, greengrocer
85 Shunn William, grocer
. *here is Little Camera street.*

87 *Britannia,* Mrs. Elizabeth Bridge
89 Bowen John, confectioner
91 Fewell Walter, fruiterer
93 Coventry Andrew, baker
93A. Goss Mrs.CarolineEleanor,grcr
    ...*here is Camera square*....
95 Robson John, lodging house
101 Richards Miss
    ..... *here is Park road*......
107 Thackeray Martin
109 Blakeman William
111 Matthews Mrs
113 Insll Thomas Edwards
115 Ellis Joseph
117 Woodward Henry
119 Underhill George William
121 Pinnell Miss
123 Oakes Alfred
125 Robinson Mrs
127 Storer & Co. carpenters
    ....*here is Fulham road*.....

EAST SIDE.
2 Randall John & Co.coal merchts
2A, Haynes Edwin, coffee house
4 *Beaufort,* John James Marsden
6 Hobbs Thomas
10 Morgan Thomas Vaughan
14 Lacon George Ovitts
16 Crisp Edwards, M.D. physician
18 Lanteri Edward
20 Hubert Adolphe, metal chaser
22 Roberts Mrs
28 Cowley William
30 Seton John William
32 Scott John Thomas
34 Roberts Robert William
36 Ruddell Henry John
38 Cave Mrs
40 Gay Mrs
    ....*here is King's road*.....
58 Mankelow Thomas, carrier
62 Issitt Alfred, china riveter
64 Hoare Thomas, carpenter
70 Powell John, bootmaker
    here is Pillar Letter Box.
  ..*here are Camera square &*
        Elm Park road......
73 Radermacher George
74 Croker Thomas William
76 Hunt Mrs
    Loveland Mrs
78 Culley Frederick
80 Ryan William, lodging house
82 Dean Mrs. Jane, lodging house
84 Edwards Mrs
86 Hervey Major William
88 Lubbock James
90 Glaister James
92 Guermonprez John Henri
94 Molyneux Miss
96 Kitchen Rev. Henry John, M.A
98 Sneed Mrs
100 Tagg Mrs.Fanny, lodging house
102 Elmsley Mrs
104 Murdstone Charles William
106 Gray Mrs. Clara, lodging house
108 Goringe George Henry, builder
    ....*here is Fulham road*.....

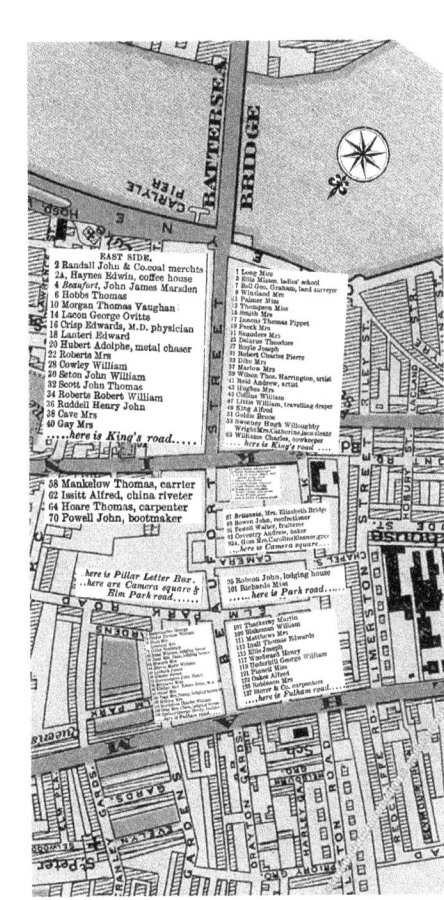

Figure 7.3 First attempt to understand the visualisation task

144 DOING DIGITAL HISTORY

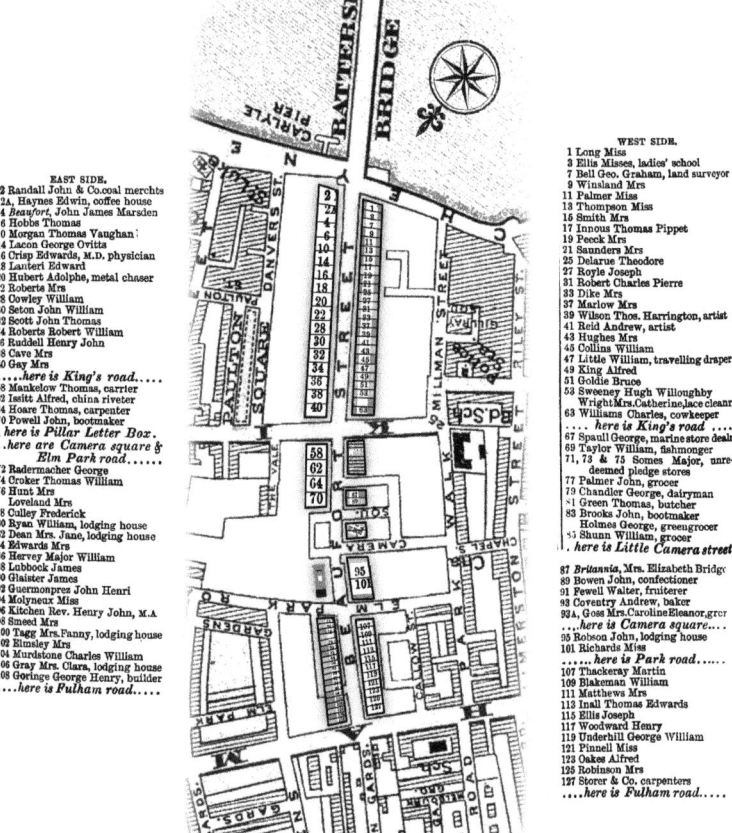

Figure 7.4 Placing indicative buildings onto the map

shadow was added, and the greyscale variant was checked to ensure that the saturation between the blue and pink was distinct enough to be identifiable, and adjusted until it was satisfactory.

Some organisation of the layers and grouping of assets in the Affinity Designer document was performed to make it easier to switch between the colour and greyscale variations of the visualisation. The mechanism of 'layers' in the application is extremely helpful in this respect, as you can make some layers visible or invisible but maintain the common layers and their common object positions.

We then continued to iterate to include additional information about the occupations, designing visual connections with outlines connecting the colour-coded buildings to the digitised text of the Post Office directory. This was to ensure that the visualisation maintained as much information as possible and linked everything together visually. Some further adjustments, such as feathering and cropping of the background maps, were applied to reinforce the focus on Beaufort Street itself; now it became possible to see which groups of buildings contained which occupations.

The next piece of information to include in the visualisation somehow was the XML data. We had already included the scanned text from the book and drawn the buildings (and got a sense of their spatial density), so including the transcribed version of each `<addr>` would be redundant and would introduce too much visual noise. However, the directory contains street markers and we had not included those, so it seemed natural and effective to integrate these XML elements into the visualisation, as a sort of 'digital background structure'. We placed text boxes of the XML snippets into the spaces between the visually connected bubbles, and included the transcription of the header, to emphasise that all the text was transcribed, not just the street markers. We deliberately used the Courier monospaced font for its old-school typewritten aesthetic, to contrast with the typography of the page scans. At this point, the visualisation was shown to and discussed with colleagues and feedback was gathered.

The final version, version 6, was then created, correcting glitches with the buildings, neatening up the document layers, visually connecting bubbles and aligning text. The layout was tightened up even more to fit the printed book page size specifications, and a legend was added in the whitespace at the top left (Figure 7.5). This position felt to us like a good and pragmatic location because the viewer will naturally see the legend as their eyes move down the pages after reading the title. They

146 DOING DIGITAL HISTORY

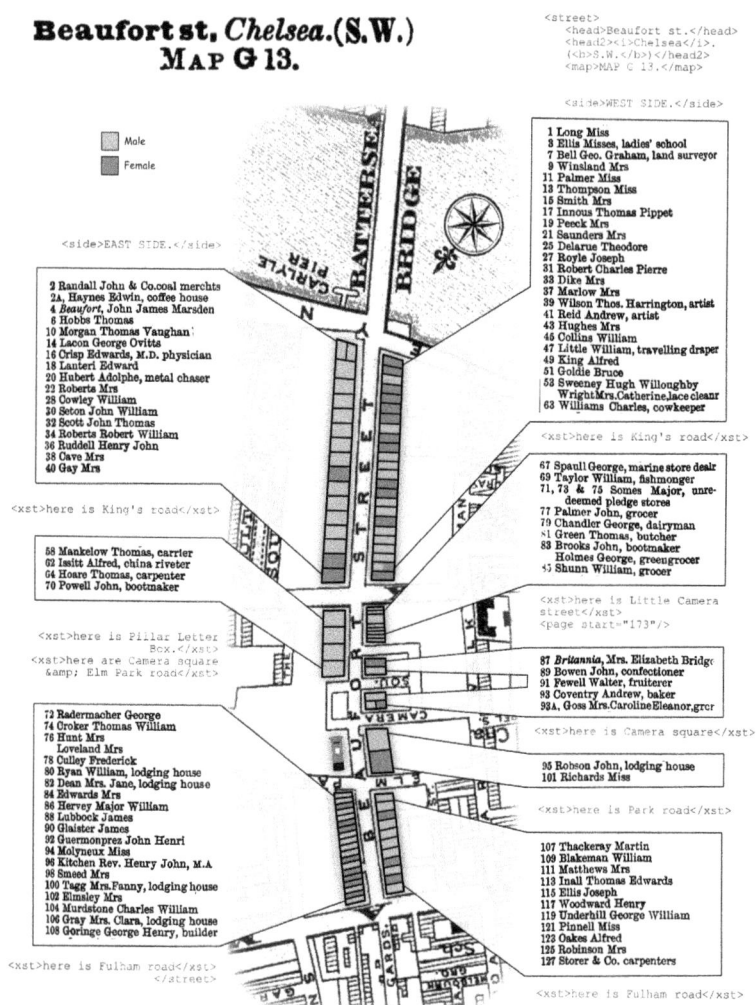

Figure 7.5 The finished visualisation in greyscale

should therefore be 'primed' to comprehend the building shapes and colours along the high street.

Again, although the print version given here is greyscale, the colour version of our visualisation is available in the book's repository, and a comparison with the printed version shows some of the compromises required in preparation of visualisations for print. We said at the beginning of the chapter that visualisation requires careful thought; we hope that, even if you do not like what we have come up with, you will agree that we spent a lot of time working on the details of our visualisation.

* * *

Throughout this book we have tried as far as possible to remain agnostic about software. That made this chapter more challenging to write than the others, but we hope that we have given you the basis with which to try visualising data yourselves. We recommend that you begin by becoming comfortable with extracting the data you want to visualise, either from our repository or from your own research, and then finding preferences in approaches and software that can produce the visualisations you find most effective.

NOTES

1. Tufte, *Envisioning Information*, p. 50 (original emphasis).
2. Tufte, *Envisioning Information*, p. 50.
3. Scott, *Seeing Like a State*, p. 3.
4. Drucker, 'Humanities approaches to graphical display'.
5. D'Ignazio and Klein, *Data Feminism*, p. 77; on viceralisation, pp. 84–91.
6. Gnuplot, www.gnuplot.info/ (accessed 11 July 2020). A very clear introduction to Gnuplot is Janert, *Gnuplot in Action*; there are also a number of online resources with examples you can copy and modify.
7. Yau, *Visualize This*.
8. Yau, *Visualize This*, p. 93.
9. The strong disagreement between statisticians over the benefits of deworming schoolchildren is a classic example of how difficult interpreting evidence can be: see Evans, 'Worm wars'.
10. Spiegelhalter, *The Art of Statistics*, p. 12.
11. Spiegelhalter, *The Art of Statistics*, p. 6.
12. Spiegelhalter's *The Art of Statistics* is a very clear general account of statistics and its pitfalls. For historians, Hudson and Ishizu's *History by Numbers* is widely used and respected.
13. Ziemann *et al.*, 'Gene name errors are widespread in the scientific literature', quoted in Liberman, 'Excel invents genes'. Some entertaining examples of Excel problems, and general problems of data types, are

given in Parker, *Humble Pi*, pp. 255–241 and 184–181 (note that the book is reverse-paginated).
14　Parker, *Humble Pi*, p. 245.
15　You can delete the closing `</addr>` tag with a simple find and replace. To delete the leading white space, we need to anchor to the beginning of the line with '`^`' then a space, and then a '`+`' to say 'one or more': find '`^ +`' and replace with nothing. The space-comma-space sequence needs to become a tab: find '` , `' (that is space-comma-space, although hard to see on the printed page!) and replace with `\t`.
16　Atkins, *The Directories of London: 1677–1977*, p. 81.
17　Spiegelhalter gives a good example of not starting axes at zero – when comparing percentages which are all very high, meaning the differences between values is obscured; see *The Art of Statistics*, p. 26.
18　Tufte, *Envisioning Information*, p. 59.
19　Hudson and Ishizu, *History by Numbers*, p. 74.
20　Yau defends pie charts in some circumstances and gives an example which is well done (see *Visualize This*, p. 141), but we are unconvinced that it is more helpful than the table he gives earlier on p. 138.
21　Edgerton, *The Shock of the Old*, p. 33.
22　Tufte, *Beautiful Evidence*, pp. 46–62 has a number of fine examples.
23　Sex Disqualification (Removal) Act 1919, www.legislation.gov.uk/ukpga/Geo5/9-10/71/section/1 (accessed 11 July 2020).
24　Vega and Vega-Lite, https://vega.github.io/ (accessed 11 July 2020).
25　See We Are Colorblind, https://wearecolorblind.com/, (accessed 11 July 2020) for discussion and examples, including links to resources that simulate colour vision deficiency so that you can test your images.
26　Chater, *The Mind is Flat*.
27　Tufte, *Beautiful Evidence*, p. 121.
28　'Economies of agglomeration', Wikipedia, https://en.wikipedia.org/wiki/Economies_of_agglomeration (accessed 11 July 2020).
29　'Bread Street', Wikipedia, https://en.wikipedia.org/wiki/Bread_Street (accessed 11 July 2020).
30　'Savile Row', Wikipedia, https://en.wikipedia.org/wiki/Savile_Row. A useful quick guide to KML is 'Help:Attached KML', Wikipedia, https://en.wikipedia.org/wiki/Help:Attached_KML (both accessed 11 July 2020).
31　ArcGIS, www.esri.com/en-us/arcgis/about-arcgis/overview (accessed 11 July 2020).
32　QGIS, www.qgis.org/en/site/ (accessed 11 July 2020).
33　MAGIS Brugge Kennisplatform (Dutch), www.magisbrugge.be/geocms/web/view/home (accessed 11 July 2020).

⇒ 8 ⇐

WHAT NEXT FOR DIGITAL HISTORY?

As we noted in the Introduction, nothing dates as quickly as predictions about the future. Consequently, we will focus here on identifying general directions of travel rather than new tools, technologies and methods. In general, we see the future of digital history as one of gradual evolution and embedding rather than of revolution and disruption. Digital methods will be more widely adopted as we gain greater access to more digital primary sources, and well-established digital tools are likely to become easier to use for a large number of researchers. This may not sound particularly exciting, but it will mark a fundamental shift in the practice of history.

BORN-DIGITAL PRIMARY SOURCES

One thing we can predict with some confidence is that historians will become increasingly concerned with born-digital sources. By 2040 the Internet Archive will have been archiving the web for more than four decades and it will be impossible to study the history of the late twentieth and early twenty-first centuries without analysing the web and social media. Libraries and archives have not yet had to deal with the 'digital deluge', but they are doing important work to prepare for it.

In the UK, the National Archives (TNA) expects that by 2021, fifty government departments will be transferring born-digital records to it routinely. To prepare for this major shift in practice, in September 2013 TNA launched a Digital Transfer Project 'to develop a scalable process for the transfer, ingest and presentation of born-digital records with long-term value; and to enable them to be held securely while closed and be accessible to the public when open'.[1] Planning on this scale is not possible for smaller libraries and archives, but they too will be receiving, cataloguing and making available born-digital materials.

There will be no overnight change in how historians work, but more and more of us will be studying so-called hybrid archives, moving between the analogue, the digital and the born digital, and acquiring the skills to make those transitions. To facilitate this, memory institutions will have to rethink how they make their collections available. Primary sources are often divided by media format in physical libraries and archives, with manuscripts in one room, rare books in another and digital collections in a third. These divisions are sometimes carried over into online catalogues and finding aids. Researchers will increasingly want to read the physical letters sent by an individual, their handwritten annotations to a book manuscript and their emails and social media. They will want to be able to do this in the same place.

We also expect the history of the digital to become an increasingly important field of digital history. This will be informed by the greater availability of born-digital sources, but it will also consider the material culture of digital technologies. It will be concerned with the political, social, cultural and economic impact of email, the internet, the web and social media. This research will be profoundly interdisciplinary, drawing on science and technology studies, media and communication studies, anthropology and ethnography as well as history. All of this will require historians to improve their digital research skills and to develop methods for effective cross- and interdisciplinary working where appropriate.

TRANSPARENCY AND OPENNESS

We have talked a lot in this book about what we see as the value of open data and the importance of openly sharing and discussing your research findings. Openness is very much on the agenda, with open science dominating discourse in Europe in particular. This has already resulted in the open publication of a great deal of secondary literature for historical research, and most digitisation projects in universities now have to make their data openly available as a condition of funding. Memory institutions have often led the way here, with initiatives like the British Library's release of a million images without copyright restrictions and the Rijksmuseum's decision in 2016 to open up its collection of digitised artworks.[2] The real value in these two initiatives lies not just in the fact that the images were published online, but that in both cases they have been published under a licence which allows downloading, reuse and manipulation without having to seek permission.

Permissive licensing is essential for digital research, we believe, and we hope that over the coming years we will see individuals, groups and institutions embracing radical openness, working in the open, sharing intellectual property, sharing knowledge and expertise.[3] For historians, this would mean being open about their own practices, including the things that have not worked, and sharing their data as a matter of course. The opportunities to do digital research would still be limited by the data that is available digitally, but the layer of constraint imposed by restrictions on reuse would be restricted. We talked in Chapter 2 about the large number of research projects that have been undertaken using Historic Hansard simply because it is open, but this will be the case for many more digitised primary sources in future.

The situation is much less clear when it comes to born-digital primary sources, many of which are subject to copyright and other restrictions on access. The drive for greater openness that we have just described will almost certainly begin to have an effect on access to these digital archives as well. There is, however, another factor to consider: much of the contemporary data that historians will want to analyse is held not by libraries and archives but by private companies which have a commercial interest in keeping that data under their control. The distorting results of this are already apparent in the field of social media research, where studies using Twitter predominate because the data is at least partially accessible. This is what happens with digitised materials too – we research what we can find – but for born-digital data the commercial imperatives are greater and ownership lies in the hands of far fewer companies.

Digital preservation specialists are working hard to ensure that digital sources will remain accessible to historians now and in the future, but while they can migrate file formats they cannot readily influence large corporations. We may lose access to important primary sources because nobody has the right or responsibility to archive them for the public good. As Viktor Mayer-Schönberger notes, 'large online platforms have become global repositories of digital memories';[4] but that is not their purpose. We envisage that libraries and archives will be empowered to begin collecting some of this previously closed-off data, and that access will gradually improve, but historians may well be required to help make the case for the importance of open digital archives.

ETHICAL RESEARCH, PRIVACY AND INCLUSIVITY

Commercial considerations can prevent access to all kinds of digital primary sources, but there is increasing discussion about the rights of the individual to decide how they want to be remembered, if indeed they want to be remembered at all. Digital methods and tools, notably search engines, mean that 'we are now able to find information which in the past would most likely have been forgotten or would have only been found by someone with very good investigative skills or significant motivation to obtain such information'.[5] Historical research is carried out by people with just that significant motivation; but given we can do so much more with digital than analogue sources, we need to stop and think about our ethical responsibilities, and not just towards the living.

Julia Laite begins a fascinating discussion of the ethical repercussions of this new way of conducting research: 'With digitized historical records now numbering in the billions, and with increasing sophistication of search technologies and machine learning, we have more and more ability to know the lives of individuals in history, even those who were humble, marginal, and obscure.'[6] Our first reaction as historians might be that this is a wonderful thing, and in many ways, of course, it is. However, 'Taking it as a given that all people want to be remembered by academic, westernized history ... is a grandiose assumption.'[7] Digital history has opened up new avenues for research and transformed the ways in which we can study both familiar and unfamiliar primary sources, but it is also making us think about the stories that we tell and how we tell them.

In the future, much greater attention will be given to how archives are constructed, by whom and what this means for historians and their research. Who is represented in the archive and how?[8] Archivists have always thought about these questions, but only in rare instances has it been a central concern for historians. This kind of re-evaluation is already happening with analogue archives, but there are particular considerations for digital history. As Laite notes, 'Users of digital resources need to understand the inequalities and power structures that built the archive; both the original archive ... and the digital one into which these records are being poured. We need to recognize the power structures of digitization itself, what this means for data, both from the past and when today's present becomes the past.'[9] We will have opportunities to research and write about previously ignored or marginalised individuals, groups and communities, to 'remember' those who have been 'forgotten', but we will increasingly have to recognise that not everyone generating data in 'today's present' wants to become part of the studied historical past.

We anticipate that people will become more conscious of their right to digital privacy, that conversations about 'the right to be forgotten' will move beyond the de-listing of information from search engines within particular geographical boundaries, and that historians will have to address the ethical questions posed by research in an increasingly digital environment. We are intrigued by Nikos Askitas's suggestion that, while digital methods help us to identify connections which reveal new information, 'As we increasingly save more data, our ability to make sense of it all will increasingly rely on techniques of forgetting such as aggregation, visualization and theory'.[10] In deriving meaning from data we may be hiding as much as we uncover. This is an important balance for historians to get right, and not something that individual researchers can be expected to establish on their own. There are many interesting discussions to be had in the coming years.

MOVING BEYOND TEXT, MOVING BEYOND SEARCH

We have noted elsewhere in this book that most of the methods we describe are for working with text rather than with still and moving image, sound or other digital media. The analysis of textual sources has always been central to historical research and, to date, digitisation initiatives have generally focused on books, manuscripts and newspapers. These do, of course, contain images, but the priority has usually been to produce machine-readable text. This has driven great improvements in OCR methods; it also explains why so much attention is now being devoted to improving tools for handwritten text recognition (HTR). Our interest in text has also led to what we could consider to be an over-reliance on keyword searching as the main technique for exploring digital materials and negotiating digital archives. As the volume of digitised data available to historians increases, keyword searching becomes less and less useful. What can you do with thirty thousand search results ranked only by the order of publication or accession into the archive? Search certainly cannot help you to determine the shape and scope of an archive or corpus. As Andrew Prescott and one of the authors of this book have noted, 'The methodological and critical issues that will be posed by the use of deep learning techniques to investigate large digital corpora have barely begun to be explored, but one thing that is clear is that use of these tools will require techniques that go beyond the simple free text search.'[11]

We expect that new ways of delineating, analysing and representing digital data will increasingly be used by historians. The growing popularity of network analysis, for example, is indicative not just of research interest in the connections between people, places and organisations but of data which is too large and complex to be viewed and presented in more traditional ways. If you cannot read everything, and keyword searching produces an overwhelming volume of results, how else can you think about analysing your sources? We already rely on search algorithms that we do not (and perhaps cannot) really understand, but we believe that greater reliance on artificial intelligence in research will require much deeper engagement with the technology. Historians will need to understand the tools that they are using, not just the sources that they are working with.

Moving away from a focus on search will also allow historians to consider non-textual primary sources to a greater extent than at present. Techniques for image searching and matching are improving all the time, and are not solely the preserve of commercial organisations. PixPlot, developed by the Yale Digital Humanities Lab, 'facilitates the dynamic exploration of tens of thousands of images' and is being used to explore and represent digital heritage collections.[12] The main objective of the Seebibyte project at the University of Oxford is to 'carry out fundamental research to develop next generation computer vision methods that are able to analyse, describe and search image and video content with human-like capabilities'.[13] It will take years before these techniques are as well developed as they are for text, but this is arguably the next big challenge for digital history.

AN ENVIRONMENTAL BACKLASH?

We hope you will forgive us for concluding this chapter with a note of caution. Much of this book has concerned how we can work with more: more text, more images, more of everything. The practice of digital history is a real-world one, and progress is dependent on sufficient investment in ongoing programmes of digitisation, on the preservation of born-digital data and on the development of new tools and platforms. But economic challenges are not the only ones with which we should be concerned.

There is a growing movement calling for people to reduce how often they fly, or even to avoid flying at all, in order to combat climate change. Researchers and academics are not immune, and the value of travelling to large international conferences, for example, is beginning to be questioned.[14] It is hard to see flying become more acceptable rather than less, and the result is likely to be an increase in digital interactions of many kinds. For historians in particular, archival research and field visits may become rarer. A trip to a distant collection may become a longer visit, where a programme of research has to be prepared well in advance. This is to hark back to research trips before the age of easy international travel, which were, of course, longer and rarer. We have already discussed Lara Putnam's concerns about the possible shallowness of online reading, and perhaps in the future historians will have to settle on a long-planned trip, 'taking time to learn about the fullness of what was going on in particular times and places, not just the fragments surfaced among search results'.[15]

But in other ways digital will become more important. Digitisation has already opened up cultural heritage to those without the resources to visit collections in person, and this may become our shared experience of research. This makes decisions about which primary sources to digitise more important than ever. It should also encourage us to think about sharing the photographs we take on those occasions when we do visit an archive. The thousands of photographs languishing on the hard drives of individual researchers are a huge untapped resource for historical research, and we hope that libraries and archives may find ways to encourage and support their sharing.

But digital tools and platforms may themselves come under increasing scrutiny. Few people think of doing an environmental audit of a website, but that may soon change. Web pages have become increasingly large over time and each download sends information, with a consequent environmental cost in terms of electricity and equipment specifications. The carbon footprint of your website may thus become an ethical issue, leading to modifications such as better optimisation of images for web delivery and local delivery of assets like video and sound. Future digitisation projects may focus less on the development of sophisticated interfaces and instead simply deliver relatively unmediated data to researchers. The Digital Archimedes Palimpsest project is a good example of this. The project website notes: 'It is important to make clear what this digital product is not. It does not come with a GUI (Graphic User Interface), and this means that it is unwieldy to use.' Instead the site acts as a data archive, and users are encouraged to take the data away: 'Please, just take it.'[16]

Maintaining and sustaining digital platforms and digital data comes with overheads, and an environmental cost, and appropriate methods for doing this will have to be worked out as we move into the third decade of the twenty-first century. For many reasons, it is an effort worth making.

NOTES

1 National Archives of the UK, 'The Digital Landscape in Government 2014–15', pp. 5–6.
2 'The British Library puts 1,000,000 images into the public domain, making them free to remix and reuse', *Open Culture* (14 December 2013), www.openculture.com/2013/12/british-library-puts-1000000-images-into-public-domain.html (accessed 11 July 2020); Baratto, 'Rijksmuseum releases 250,000 images of artwork for free download'.
3 See Tapscott and Williams, *Radical Openness: Four Unexpected Principles for Success* (TED conferences, 2013). We owe this reference to Teal Triggs.
4 Mayer-Schönberger, 'Remembering (to) delete: forgetting beyond informational privacy', in Thouvenin *et al.*, eds, *Remembering and Forgetting in the Digital Age*, p. 118.
5 Thouvenin, 'Search engines', in Thouvenin *et al.*, eds, *Remembering and Forgetting in the Digital Age*, p. 64.
6 Laite, 'The emmet's inch', 2.
7 Laite, 'The emmet's inch', 17.
8 Risam, *New Digital Worlds*, pp. 47–64.
9 Laite, 'The emmet's inch', 19.
10 Askitas, 'On the interplay between forgetting and remembering', in Thouvenin *et al.*, eds, *Remembering and Forgetting*, p. 144.
11 Winters and Prescott, 'Negotiating the born-digital', 399.
12 PixPlot, http://dhlab.yale.edu/projects/pixplot/ (accessed 11 July 2020).
13 Seebibyte: Visual Search for the Era of Big Data, http://seebibyte.org/ (accessed 11 July 2020).
14 Gerhards, '"Greetings from Berlin, Tokyo, Berlin"'.
15 Putnam, 'The transnational and the text-searchable', 401.
16 The Digital Archimedes Palimpsest, http://archimedespalimpsest.org/digital/ (accessed 11 July 2020).

TEST YOURSELF ANSWERS

These are possible answers to the quizzes at the end of chapters 4 and 5. They are not definitive: there are often multiple ways to get the required result.

CHAPTER 4

1. To find subdivided properties, we want any letter after the number, which we can find either by adding the character class [A-Za-z]: to our previous grep:

    ```
    grep -E "^[0-9]+[A-Za-z]" Balls-Pond-road.txt
    ```

    This returns one property, 134A, where a cabinet maker is listed. We can also make grep case insensitive with the -i flag:

    ```
    grep -Ei "^[0-9]+[a-z]" Balls-Pond-road.txt
    ```

    This returns the same result with a bit less typing.

2. Because using the *.txt syntax aggregates all the results from the text files, the distinction between files will be lost. You can operate on all files in a directory one by one by creating a 'loop'. That is beyond the scope of this book, but a web search for 'bash loop' will show the syntax for this.

    ```
    grep -Ev "^[0-9]" *.txt | less
    ```

3. To filter out the cross streets, you can pipe one grep -v to another. This is a quick way to test some regular expressions. However, it is

158 TEST YOURSELF ANSWERS

much easier to write the results of this command to a new file called, say, unnumbered-addresses.txt:

```
grep -Ev "^[0-9]" *.txt > unnumbered-addresses.txt
```

You can then clean the file up with a mixture of regex and manual deletions.

CHAPTER 5

1.
   ```
   grep -E "\bMrs\b" all-b-streets.xml |grep -Eo
   ",[^,]+<" | sort | uniq -c | sort -nr | less
   grep -E "\bMiss\b" all-b-streets.xml |grep -Eo
   ",[^,]+<" | sort | uniq -c | sort -nr | less
   ```

   This was our solution but it can probably be improved upon.

2. By definition, this is your choice, but here is a single address from Bacon Street which we have marked up more fully:

   ```
   <addr>
   <property number="5" type="residential">5
   </property>
   <name gender="male">
   <surname>Holding</surname>
   <firstname>Alfred</firstname>
   </name>,
   <occupation type="artisan"
   material="wood">chairmaker
   </occupation>
   </addr>
   ```

3. With markup added, you can grep for the opening tag, followed by any text, followed by the opening tag. For example, this will list all of the occupations:

   ```
   grep -Eo "<occupation.+</occupation>" filename.xml
   ```

APPENDIX 1: GETTING THE DATA

We strongly recommend trying out the techniques we describe in the book, particularly for sorting, searching and cleaning data. In many ways it is optimal to use your own work for this, but you may not have data that you can work with. Or you may try something and get stuck because your format is slightly different and the commands will not work exactly as described.

We have put the data files you will need to follow along into an open repository on GitHub at https://github.com/ihr-digital/digital-history. On this page you will see a listing of the directory structure of the repository, and below that you will see explanatory text which is derived from the README.md file, which you will also see in the file listing.

At the time of writing there is a green button on the right of the screen labelled 'Clone or download'. This gives you either the URL to clone using Git or a link to download the repository as a zip file. We would suggest you use the Git method for the practice. As long as you have Git installed (see Chapter 4), you just need to type at the command line:

```
git clone https://github.com/ihr-digital/digital-history
```

Git will then copy the directory structure of our repository into a folder on your computer called digital-history. But please note that Git will do this in the location at which your command prompt is when you type the command (you can check this by typing pwd). For using the repository locally, it does not matter where you put it, but if you would prefer it elsewhere then you can move it in the same way you would move any folder around.

If you would rather not clone you can download a zip file and unzip it where you choose.

However you got the data, now have a look around the folder. Most of the files we will be working on are in data. Use cd until the result of typing pwd ends in:

```
/digital-history/data
```

What comes before the first slash of course depends on your local file structure, but when you are in the right place you are ready to go.

Remember that you can experiment with these files without worrying about messing anything up. Indeed, we would encourage you to see what happens when you do mistakenly delete or overwrite a few of these files. When you go through the section on Git in Chapter 6 please do try out the commands here. At any point, you can either use `git checkout .` to reset the repository or even clone the repository again from scratch.

APPENDIX 2: SOME COMMAND LINE RECIPES

Note that for brevity here we have generally described commands as working on a file or files. Commands with no example usage given can be used with no arguments. Nearly all of these commands work equally on other output, which often comes from a pipe but need not do.

Table A2.1 Some command line recipes

What it does	Command	Example
Navigation		
print working directory – tells you where you are in the file system	`pwd`	
change directory – move to your home folder	`cd`	
move to the specified folder	`cd name`	`cd Documents/data`
move up one or more levels	`cd ..`	`cd ../..`
list files in the working folder	`ls`	`ls *.txt`
list long – detailed listing of files in the working folder	`ls -l`	`ls -l *.pdf`
make directory – create a folder with the specified name	`mkdir`	`mkdir new-project`
Finding and inspecting		
concatenate – print a file or files to screen	`cat`	`cat notes.txt`
combine multiple files	`cat`	`cat *.txt > combined.txt`

Table A2.1 Continued

What it does	Command	Example
find files with this name within the current folder or any subfolders	find . -name	find . -name *.mp3
show the first ten lines of the specified files	head	head *.xml
show the first three lines from each CSV in a directory		head -n 3 *.csv
word count for lines, words and characters in a file	wc	wc *.csv
sort a file	sort	sort list.txt
sort a file in reversed numeric order		sort -nr list.txt
list lines without showing duplicates	uniq	sort | uniq
list lines without showing duplicates but with a count for duplicates lines	uniq -c	sort | uniq -c
Moving		
copy files to a new location or in place	cp	cp old.txt new.txt cp *.txt new-project/
move files to a new location or rename in place	mv	mv old.txt new.txt mv *.txt new-project/
remove files completely	rm	rm *.csv
remove files but check each one before deletion	rm -i	rm -i *.csv
Slicing and dicing		
return lines containing a string	grep	grep "needle" haystack.txt

Appendix 2: Some Command Line Recipes

Table A2.1 Continued

What it does	Command	Example
produce a unique list of elements and attributes in an XML document		`grep -Eo "<[^/>]+>" filename.xml | sort | uniq`
as above but lists only elements, not attributes		`grep -Eo "<[^ />" /filename/.xml | sort | uniq`
return a particular column	cut	`cut -f1 myfile.csv`
extract the second column from a CSV file		`cut -d, -f2 myfile.csv`
Comparing		
compare two sorted lists	comm	`comm file-a.txt file-b.txt`
list items in file 'a' which are not in file 'b'		`comm -23 file-a.txt file-b.txt`
display differences between two files	diff	`diff file-a.txt file-b.txt`
print the hash of a file	md5sum	`md5sum file1.tif`
list duplicate files (in this case tiffs)		`md5sum *.tif | sort | uniq -d`
Manipulating		
replace one character with another	tr	`tr '1' '2' < file.xml`
change all instances of 'house' to 'garden' and print the result	sed	`sed 's/house/garden/g' novel.txt`
change all instances of 'house' to 'garden' in the original file		`sed -i 's/house/garden/g' novel.txt`
change all instances of 'house' to 'garden' in all text files in the folder, but make a back-up of each original file		`sed -i.bak 's/house/garden/g' *.txt`

APPENDIX 2: SOME COMMAND LINE RECIPES

Table A2.1 Continued

What it does	Command	Example
Git		
report on files' status (if they are staged or tracked)	`git status`	
show details of previous commits	`git log`	
add a file to stage	`git add`	`git add README.md`
add all modified files to stage		`git add .`
commit all staged files (a commit message is mandatory)	`git commit -m`	`git commit -m "added bibliographic references"`
revert a file to its state at last commit	`git checkout`	`git checkout chapter1.txt`
revert the whole folder to an earlier commit (use the beginning of that commit's hash)		`git checkout a9aadf8`
push the latest local commits to a remote repository	`git push`	`git push origin`
pull the latest commits from a remote repository	`git pull`	`git pull origin`
Miscellaneous		
list previous command	`history`	`history	grep "cut"`
print a file with the lines randomly ordered	`shuf`	`shuf -n 10 lottery.txt`
print a calendar	`cal`	
print the calendar for October 1552		`cal 10 1552`
compute historic dates	`ncal`	
print the date of Easter Day in 1213		`ncal -e 1213`

APPENDIX 3: REGULAR EXPRESSIONS

This is a summary of the fundamentals of basic expressions. There are a few more exotic pieces of syntax available, but we use those so rarely ourselves that we think including them here would be unhelpful. If your needs go beyond what is listed here, we suggest referring to *Mastering Regular Expressions* by Jeffrey Friedl.

Table A3.1 Summary of regular expression characters

Quantifiers	Special characters
+ (one or more of the preceding) ? (one or none of the preceding) * (zero or more of the preceding)	. (any character) \n (line break) \t (tab) \b (word boundary)
Anchors	**Character classes**
^ (beginning of the line) $ (end of the line)	Enclosing anything within square brackets [] means 'any one of these' Negate with an initial ^, e.g. [^;]
Back references	**Escaping**
Enclose any elements you want remembered in parentheses ( ). A few editors use \(and \).	The following special characters need to be preceded by \ to make them literal: $^.[]+?*\ So to search for a literal ? you need \? and so on.
Refer back to the parentheses, in left to right order, as $1, $2 and so on. A few editors use \1 and \2, or \\1, \\2, etc.	For most editors, parentheses also need to be escaped

REFERENCES

Atkins, Peter J., *The Directories of London, 1677–1977* (London: Continuum International Publishing, 1990).

Ayers, Edward L., 'The Pasts and Futures of Digital History', www.vcdh.vir ginia.edu/PastsFutures.html (accessed 8 July 2020).

Baratto, Romullo, 'Rijksmuseum releases 250,000 images of artwork for free download', *ArchDaily* (1 July 2016), www.archdaily.com/790578/ rijksmuseum-releases-250000-free-images-of-artwork-for-download (accessed 11 July 2020).

Barney, Stephen A., ed., *The Etymologies of Isidore of Seville* (New York: Cambridge University Press, 2010).

Berry, David M., *The Philosophy of Software: Code and Mediation in the Digital Age* (Basingstoke: Palgrave Macmillan, 2015).

Berry, David M. and Fagerjord, Anders, *Digital Humanities: Knowledge and Critique in a Digital Age* (Cambridge: Polity, 2017).

Blair, Ann, *Too Much to Know: Managing Scholarly Information before the Modern Age* (New Haven and London: Yale University Press, 2011).

Blaney, Jonathan, 'Introduction to the principles of linked open data', *Programming Historian* (7 May 2017), https://programminghistorian. org/en/lessons/intro-to-linked-data (accessed 5 July 2020).

Blaney, Jonathan and Siefring, Judith, 'A culture of non-citation: assessing the digital impact of British History Online and the Early English Books Online Text Creation Partnership', *Digital Humanities Quarterly*, 11.1 (2016), no pagination.

Bodard, Gabriel, 'Scanning and printing a Greek vase' (blog), *Institute of Classical Studies* (15 January 2018), https://ics.blogs.sas.ac.uk/2018/ 01/15/scanning-and-printing-a-greek-vase/ (accessed 8 July 2020).

Braudel, Fernand, *Écrits sur l'histoire* (Paris: Flammarion, 1969).

Brown, John Seely and Duguid, Paul, *The Social Life of Information* (Boston: Harvard Business Review Press, 2000).

Brügger, Niels and Milligan, Ian, *The SAGE Handbook of Web History* (Los Angeles: SAGE, 2018).

Brügger, Niels and Schroeder, Ralph, *The Web as History: Using Web Archives to Understand the Past and the Present* (London: UCL Press, 2017), available open access at www.uclpress.co.uk/collections/media-studies/products/84067 (accessed 8 July 2020).

Bush, Vannevar, 'As we may think', *The Atlantic* (July 1945), www.theatlantic.com/magazine/archive/1945/07/as-we-may-think/303881/ (accessed 8 July 2020).

Carr, Nicholas G., *The Shallows: How the Internet Is Changing the Way We Think, Read and Remember* (London: Atlantic Books, 2010).

Chacon, Scott and Straub, Ben, *Pro Git*, 2nd edition (New York: Apress, 2014), https://git-scm.com/book/en/v2 (accessed 10 July 2020).

Chater, Nick, *The Mind Is Flat: The Illusion of Mental Depth and the Improvised Mind* (London: Allen Lane, 2018).

Cohen, Daniel J., 'From Babel to knowledge: data mining large digital collections', *D-Lib Magazine*, 12.3 (2006), https://doi.org/10.1045/march2006-cohen.

Conrad, Alfred Haskell and Meyer, John Robert, *The Economics of Slavery: And Other Studies in Econometric History* (Chicago: Aldine Publishing Company, 1964).

Corens, Liesbeth, Peters, Kate and Walsham, Alexandra, eds, *Archives and Information in the Early Modern World*, Proceedings of the British Academy, 212 (Oxford: Oxford University Press, 2018).

Crawford, Matthew, *The World Beyond Your Head: How to Flourish in an Age of Distraction* (London: Viking, 2015).

Crompton, Constance, Lane, Richard and Siemens, Raymond, eds, *Doing Digital Humanities: Practice, Training, Research* (London: Routledge, 2016).

Darnton, Robert, 'A program for reviving the monograph', *Perspectives on History* (1 March 1999), www.historians.org/publications-and-directories/perspectives-on-history/march-1999/a-program-for-reviving-the-monograph (accessed 8 July 2020).

Dictionary of National Biography on CD-ROM (Oxford: Oxford University Press, 1995).

D'Ignazio, Catherine and Klein, Lauren F., *Data Feminism* (Cambridge, MA: MIT Press: 2020).

Dourish, Paul, *The Stuff of Bits: An Essay on the Materialities of Information* (Cambridge, MA: MIT Press: 2017).

Drucker, Johanna, 'Humanities approaches to graphical display', *Digital Humanities Quarterly*, 5.1 (2011), www.digitalhumanities.org/dhq/vol/5/1/000091/000091.html (accessed 12 November 2020).

Edgerton, David, *The Shock of the Old: Technology and Global History Since 1900* (Oxford: Oxford University Press, 2007).

Evans, David, 'Worm wars: the anthology', *Development Impact*, World Bank blogs (4 August 2015), http://blogs.worldbank.org/impactevalua tions/worm-wars-anthology (accessed 11 July 2020).

Friedl, Jeffrey M., *Mastering Regular Expressions*, 3rd edition (Sebastopol: O'Reilly, 2006).

Gartner, Richard, *Metadata: Shaping Knowledge from Antiquity to the Semantic Web* (Cham, Switzerland: Springer International, 2016).

Gawande, Atul, 'Why doctors hate their computers', *New Yorker* (5 November 2018), 62–73.

Gentzkow, Matthew, Kelly, Bryan T. and Taddy, Matt, 'Text as data', *Journal of Economic Literature*, 57.3 (2019), 535–574, https://doi.org/10.1257/jel.20181020.

Gerhards, Jürgen, '"Greetings from Berlin, Tokyo, Beijing" – should we call time on international academic travel?', *LSE Impact Blog* (25 February 2019), https://blogs.lse.ac.uk/impactofsocialsciences/2019/02/25/greetings-from-berlin-tokyo-beijing-should-we-call-time-on-interna tional-academic-travel/ (accessed 11 July 2020).

Gold, Matthew and Klein, Lauren, eds, *Debates in the Digital Humanities 2016* (Minneapolis: University of Minnesota Press, 2016), https://doi.org/10.5749/9781452963761.

Grafton, Anthony, *The Footnote: A Curious History* (London: Faber, 1997).

———, *Worlds Made by Words: Scholarship and Community in the Modern West* (Cambridge, MA: Harvard University Press, 2009).

Greengrass, Mark and Hughes, Lorna M., eds, *The Virtual Representation of the Past* (Farnham: Ashgate, 2008).

Haggerty, John and Haggerty, Sheryllynne, 'The life cycle of a metropolitan business network: Liverpool 1750–1810', *Explorations in Economic History*, 48.2 (2011), 189–206, https://doi.org/10.1016/j.eeh.2010.09.006.

Hedges, Mark and Dunn, Stuart, 'Crowd-Sourcing Scoping Study: Engaging the Crowd with Humanities Research' (London: Arts and Humanities Research Council, 2012), https://kclpure.kcl.ac.uk/portal/files/5786937/Crowdsourcing_connected_communities.pdf (accessed 5 July 2020).

Hill, Mark J. and Hengchen, Simon, 'Quantifying the impact of dirty OCR on historical text analysis: Eighteenth Century Collections Online as a case study', *Digital Scholarship in the Humanities*, 34.4 (2019), 825–843 https://doi.org/10.1093/llc/fqz024.

Hitchcock, Tim, 'Confronting the digital, or how academic history writing lost the plot', *Cultural and Social History*, 10.1 (2013), 9–23, https://doi.org/10.2752/147800413X13515292098070.

———, 'Digital affordances for criminal justice history', *Crime, History and Societies*, 21.2 (2017), 335–342.

Holley, Rose, 'How good can it get? Analysing and improving OCR accuracy in large scale historic newspaper digitisation programs', *D-Lib Magazine*, 15.3/4 (2009), https://doi.org/10.1045/march2009-holley.

Hudson, Pat and Ishizu, Mina, *History by Numbers: An Introduction to Quantitative Approaches*, 2nd edition (London: Bloomsbury, 2017).

Janert, Philipp K., *Gnuplot in Action*, 2nd edition (Shelter Island: Manning Publications, 2015).

Laite, Julia, 'The emmet's inch: small history in a digital age', *Journal of Social History* (online first), https://doi.org/10.1093/jsh/shy118.

Le Roy Ladurie, Emmanuel, *Le territoire de l'historien* (Paris: Gallimard, 1973).

Levy, Steven, 'A spreadsheet way of knowledge', *Backchannel* (24 October 2014), https://medium.com/backchannel/a-spreadsheet-way-of-knowledge-8de60af7146e (accessed 8 July 2020).

Liberman, Mark 'Excel invents genes', *Language Log* (26 August 2016), https://languagelog.ldc.upenn.edu/nll/?p=27730 (accessed 11 July 2020).

Licklider, J. C. R., *Libraries of the Future* (Cambridge, MA: MIT Press, 1965).

Milligan, Ian, 'Illusionary order: online databases, optical character recognition, and Canadian history, 1997–2010', *Canadian Historical Review*, 94.4 (2013), 540–569.

———, 'Lost in the infinite archive: the promise and pitfalls of web archives', *International Journal of Humanities and Arts Computing*, 10 (2016), 78–94, https://doi.org/10.3366/ijhac.2016.0161.

Montgomery, Guy, Jackman, Mary and Agoa, Helen S., eds, *Concordance to the Poetical Works of John Dryden* (New York: Russell & Russell, 1967).

National Archives of the UK, 'The Digital Landscape in Government 2014–15: Business Intelligence Review' (London: National Archives of the UK, 2016), www.nationalarchives.gov.uk/documents/digital-landscape-in-government-2014-15.pdf (accessed 11 July 2020).

Newport, Cal, *Digital Minimalism: On Living Better with Less Technology* (London: Penguin, 2019).

Noble, Safiya Umoja, *Algorithms of Oppression: How Search Engines Reinforce Racism* (New York: New York University Press, 2018).

O'Neil, Cathy, *Weapons of Math Destruction: How Big Data Increases Inequality and Threatens Democracy* (London: Penguin, 2017).

Osterberg, Gayle, 'Update on the Twitter archive at the Library of Congress', *Library of Congress Blog* (26 December 2017), https://blogs.loc.gov/loc/2017/12/update-on-the-twitter-archive-at-the-library-of-congress-2/?loclr=blogloc (accessed 8 July 2020).

Parker, Matt, *Humble Pi: A Comedy of Maths Errors* (London: Allen Lane, 2019).

Pons, Anaclet, *El desorden digital. Guía para historiadores y humanistas* (Madrid: Siglo XXI, 2015).

Putnam, Lara, 'The transnational and the text-searchable: digitized sources and the shadows they cast', *American Historical Review*, 121.2 (2016), 377–402.

Raulff, Ulrich, *Farewell to the Horse: The Final Century of Our Relationship*, trans. by Ruth Ahmedzai Kemp (London: Allen Lane, 2017).

Risam, Roopika, *New Digital Worlds: Postcolonial Digital Humanities in Theory, Practice, and Pedagogy* (Evanston: Northwestern University Press, 2018).

Sassone, Peter G., 'Survey finds low office productivity linked to staffing imbalances', *National Productivity Review*, 11.2 (1992), 147–158, https://doi.org/10.1002/npr.4040110203.

Schafer, Valérie, Truc, Gérôme, Badouard, Romain, Castex, Lucien and Musiani, Francesca, 'Paris and Nice terrorist attacks: exploring Twitter and web archives', *Media, War and Conflict* (3 April 2019), https://doi.org/10.1177/1750635219839382.

Scott, James C., *Seeing Like a State: How Certain Schemes to Improve the Human Condition Have Failed* (New Haven: Yale University Press, 1998).

Siefring, Judith and Meyer, Eric T., 'Sustaining the EEBO-TCP Corpus in Transition: Report on the TIDSR Benchmarking Study' (Rochester: Social Science Research Network, 2013), https://papers.ssrn.com/abstract=2236202 (accessed 8 July 2020).

Spence, Ian, 'Playfair, William (1759–1823)', *Oxford Dictionary of National Biography*' (Oxford: Oxford University Press, n.d.), https://doi.org/10.1093/ref:odnb/22370.

Spiegelhalter, David, *The Art of Statistics: Learning from Data* (London: Pelican Books, 2019).

Suber, Peter, *Open Access* (Cambridge, MA, and London: MIT Press, 2012), available open access at www.dropbox.com/s/5cxsyzs58a5yx5q/9286.pdf?dl=0 (accessed 19 July 2020).

Swartz, Nikki, 'UK puts parliament proceedings online', *Information Management Journal*, 42.4 (2008), 7.

Tamm, Marek and Burke, Peter, eds, *Debating New Approaches to History* (London: Bloomsbury Academic, 2018).

Tanner, Simon, Muñoz, Trevor and Ros, Pich Hemy, 'Measuring mass text digitization, quality and usefulness: lessons learned from assessing the OCR accuracy of the British Library's 19th Century Online Newspaper Archive', *D-Lib Magazine*, 15.7/8 (2009), www.dlib.org/dlib/july09/munoz/07munoz.html (accessed 5 July 2020).

Tapscott, Don and Williams, Anthony D., *Radical Openness: Four Unexpected Principles for Success* (New York: TED Conferences, 2013).

Thomas, David, Fowler, Simon and Johnson, Valerie, *The Silence of the Archive* (London: Facet Publishing, 2017).

Thouvenin, Florent, Hettich, Peter and Burkert, Herbert, *Remembering and Forgetting in the Digital Age* (New York: Springer, 2018).

Tufte, Edward R., *Envisioning Information* (Cheshire, CT: Graphics Press, 1990).

———, *Beautiful Evidence* (Cheshire, CT: Graphics Press, 2006).

Veyne, Paul, *Les grecs, ont-ils cru à leur mythes?: essai sur l'imagination constituante* (Paris: Seuil, 1983).

Vice, John and Farrell, Stephen, *The History of Hansard* (London: House of Lords Hansard and the House of Lords Library, 2015).

Winters, Jane and Prescott, Andrew, 'Negotiating the born-digital: a problem of search', *Archives and Manuscripts*, 47 (2019), 391–403, https://doi.org/10.1080/01576895.2019.1640753.

Wolf, Maryanne, *Reader, Come Home: The Reading Brain in a Digital World* (New York: Harper, 2018).

Yau, Nathan, *Visualize This: The Flowing Data Guide to Design, Visualization, and Statistics* (Indianapolis: John Wiley & Sons, 2011).

Ziemann, Mark, Eren, Yotam and El-Osta, Assam, 'Gene name errors are widespread in the scientific literature', *Genome Biology*, 17 (2016), 177, https://doi.org/10.1186/s13059-016-1044-7.

Zuboff, Shoshana, *The Age of Surveillance Capitalism* (London: Profile Books, 2019).

INDEX

| 82–85, 95

Affinity Designer 142
Anglo-American Legal Tradition 30–31
Annales school 8
API *see* application programming interface
application programming interface 36–37
attributes 101–103

bar charts 7, 131–133
Bibliography of British and Irish History 14
big data 11
Busa, Roberto 7–8
Bush, Vannevar 13

citation 20–22
climate change 154–156
cliometrics 8
colour 137–138
command line 70–74
Conrad, Alfred 8
Creative Commons 120–121
crowdsourcing 34–35

data cleaning 54–56
data management 107–109
data sharing 118–121
digital humanities 6–8
documentation 116–117

EEBO *see* Early English Books Online
Early English Books Online 6–7
Excel *see* Microsoft Excel

find and replace 68–69
Floud, Roderick 8–9

geocoding 140
Geographic Information System 139–140
georectification 140–141
Gephi 10–11
GIS *see* Geographic Information System
Git 111–116
Global Position System 138
Google 17
Google Books 15
Google Maps 139–140
GPS *see* Global Position System
grep 75–87, 92–99, 128–130

handwritten text recognition 35–36
Hansard 28–30
Henry III Fine Rolls Project 33
histograms 132–133
History and Computing 9
HTR *see* handwritten text recognition
hybrid archives 150

Internet Archive 12

INDEX 173

keyword search *see* search

Le Roy Ladurie, Emmanuel 8

maps 138–146
Mendenhall, T. C. 7
metadata 41, 109
Meyer, John 8
Microsoft Excel 9–10, 127–130
Microsoft Word 9–10
Miles, Josephine 7

network analysis 10–11, 19, 154
newspapers 27, 31–33

OCR *see* optical character recognition
Old Bailey Online 36–37
open data 28–29, 43–44, 150–151
optical character recognition 31–34, 52–55

pie charts 7, 131–132
pipe *see* |
plain text 60–61
Playfair, William 7
Post Office directory for London 48–50
precision 17
privacy 152–153
publication 42–44

quantifiers 68

Raspberry Pi 62
raster graphics 142

RDF *see* Resource Description Framework
recall 17
regex *see* regular expressions
regular expressions 55–57, 63–69, 75–87, 94–99
research ethics 152–156
Resource Description Framework 38
Royal Historical Society Bibliography see *Bibliography of British and Irish History*

scanning 51–52
search 15–18, 153–154
sparklines 133
stacked bar charts 134–136
statistics 126

TEI *see* Text Encoding Initiative
Text Encoding Initiative 103–104
Transcribe Bentham 35
Twitter 12, 59–60

vector graphics 142
version control 110–111

web archiving 12–13, 39–40
websites 119
Word *see* Microsoft Word

XML 90–104

EU authorised representative for GPSR:
Easy Access System Europe, Mustamäe tee 50,
10621 Tallinn, Estonia
gpsr.requests@easproject.com

www.ingramcontent.com/pod-product-compliance
Ingram Content Group UK Ltd.
Pitfield, Milton Keynes, MK11 3LW, UK
UKHW021837140426
5217IPUK00022B/1496